THE *NEW*

PERFECT

RESUME

THE NEW PERFECT RESUME

Tom Jackson
AND
Ellen Jackson

MAIN
STREET
BOOKS

DOUBLEDAY

NEW YORK   LONDON   TORONTO   SYDNEY   AUCKLAND

A MAIN STREET BOOK

PUBLISHED BY DOUBLEDAY
a division of Bantam Doubleday Dell Publishing Group, Inc.
1540 Broadway, New York, New York 10036

MAIN STREET BOOKS, DOUBLEDAY, and the portrayal of a building with a tree are
trademarks of Doubleday, a division of Bantam Doubleday Dell Publishing
Group, Inc.

Library of Congress Cataloging-in-Publication Data

Jackson, Tom.
    [Perfect resume]
    The new perfect resume / Tom Jackson.
        p. cm.
    Originally published: The perfect resume, 1980.
    Includes bibliographical references and indexes.
    1. Resumes (Employment)   2. Applications for positions.
  I.   Title.
  HF5383.J25   1996
  808'.06665—dc20   96-12401
                                                     CIP

ISBN 0-385-48190-X

Printed in the United States of America

September 1996
Text design by Stanley S. Drate/Folio Graphics Co. Inc.

10   9   8   7

Contents

A Report from the Front Lines

The Perfect Resume could not be revised and reissued in the mid-1990s without looking at the resume's overall future life span.

Since this book was first published in 1980, there have been at least fifty more resume books published. For a fresh look we ask ourselves again: What exactly is the *perfect* resume? The answer is the same: The perfect resume is the one that gets you called in for an interview.

The *new* perfect resume is more subtle to describe, for the additive menu is varied—fax, E-mail, Internet, video, diskette, or any combination of these. Still, most employers today prefer to read attractive, clean, clearly written paper resumes. The strength of honest, clean writing that gives the reader what is important to know is irreversible. Thank goodness.

As a way to revisit the resume before it becomes obsolete in its current form, we interviewed a few employers, placement counselors, and other experts in the field of managing change.

Question: *When you have to hire (or recruit), how effective are today's resumes in pinpointing the right people to call in for interviews?*

Three out of four of our experts agreed that the biggest problems with today's resumes are an overstating of qualifications and a vagueness of actual skills. Competencies claims are not specifically backed up with results or achievements. Although resumes are shorter and somewhat better focused, it's still hard work to read between the lines.

Question: *Should people emphasize experience, competencies, or both, and in what proportion?*

Three out of four, again, valued experience over competencies. This means experience as in specific results, not just history. Bottom line: No matter how the information is arranged the accomplishments or results must describe the competency in action.

Question: *For what purposes and how effective is the use of nontraditional resumes—fax, E-mail, scanned, video, Internet, diskette?*

No one was averse to the nontraditional resumes, but everyone still wants and prefers the standard paper copy. All agreed that video resumes work well for salespeople or other presentation/platform skills requirements; diskettes are great for designers and graphic artists; fax and E-mail are good for a first cut when time is of the essence; the Internet—well, yes, maybe sometimes. But always, always, *always* back these up with a paper copy.

Question: *What advice would you give a new graduate in entering the job market and making a good presentation?*

Everyone agreed that a new graduate had to make nonwork or part-time work experience translatable in terms of specific skills, both on the resume and in the interview. New grads also need to demonstrate a willingness, even a passion, for learning and a commitment to working hard through any work challenge. Especially in interviews, they need to distinguish themselves from the crowd, to sell their uniqueness.

Question: *How do you discuss job security in an interview?*

No one disputes that job security is now obsolete. Career self-management with personal responsibility is called for everywhere. The best employers, however, do not use this theme to let people float in a fog. Any company that hopes to compete keeps an eye on providing employees with opportunities for skills development, industry knowledge, and personal balance. Smart job seekers know better than to even ask about job security.

Question: *In interviews, what are the most important qualities you seek in hiring new talent?*

Everyone put resiliency/flexibility at the top. Second was leadership/initiative. All other answers were derivative of the first two.

So what does this all mean to you? If you have read any earlier version of *The Perfect Resume*, you'll find this revision different in some key areas. In the early chapters you'll dive more deeply into how to translate the new work rules into an attitude for redirecting, reinventing, and reenergizing your work so that you are more resourceful than ever before in having work that lets you grow and flourish, professionally and financially.

We've upgraded our worksheets and placed them all together in the second section of the book. You can read the first section now as its own separate treatment. When you're ready to get down to work, you'll go right to the worksheets section, photocopy extra sheets if you want, or even copy the forms onto your word processor.

We've now addressed internal job development, with its focus on capability or competency. We've given more specific help with cover letter worksheets, and we've doubled our number of sample resumes, which are now in the third section—the Resume Catalog.

In the back of the book are several pages of bibliography covering jobs, careers, and the whole worklife revolution.

So have fun. Use the book any way you wish. Take with you all those parts that make sense to you and leave behind the rest. The only truly perfect resume is the one that works for you.

SECTION ONE

THE

BIG

PICTURE

Reinventing Your Future

Your future worklife is a voyage and you are at the helm. Today, the seas are turbulent. Global competition demands that business leaders and managers rethink the way their organizations are run from top to bottom. The imperative to focus on customers—to give them what they want when they want it, and at prices they are willing to pay—means that companies must redesign, reengineer, and reinvent the way their best possible work is accomplished.

Today, opportunities for employment are unpredictable, shrinking in number and changing in nature in ways that will affect everyone. The whole idea of "career," as previously understood, is dead. To some degree every job is at risk. This is especially true at highly competitive, quickly evolving organizations. As companies adapt to changing needs and technologies, downsizing is inevitable, putting at risk everyone and every job, from executive suite to factory floor.

This leaves many people adrift and struggling to survive in an ocean of change. First, we must find the life raft; then, once we understand the frequency and size of the waves, we can switch to the surfboard. It is only with agility, versatility, and quick-wittedness that we will stay on top. We literally *must*, personally and individually, reinvent our future.

The stakes are high: With the dramatic changes in virtually every kind of enterprise, our livelihood, freedom of movement, and personal fulfillment depend on exercising imagination, courage, and the highest quality thinking.

THE CHANGING AMERICAN WORKPLACE

For decades the United States exported its homegrown inventions and ideas. Our product-based industries, technology, and consumer society fueled both commercial and cultural growth all over the world.

In more recent years, traditional American progress declined. What we once believed were unlimited resources became scarce, eaten up by national debt, business failures, and large social programs. Many American companies have found themselves too fat, too costly, and, in many cases, too bureaucratic. One by one, foreign competitors grabbed chunks of our biggest markets: cars, steel, electronics, global finance.

Today, we see an upswing in the resurgence of American inventiveness and an improvement in productivity. The creation of new jobs is part of this rebirth of American business. There is now an open job market. Employment security as a company benefit is gone. Employability now depends on the individual's constant and active adaptation to change. People are being asked to *learn* and to *change* or to *leave*.

No longer do companies assume responsibility for their employees' future. As coldhearted as it sounds, unless a job is essential in providing value to the customer, it is in jeopardy. The companies that don't learn this lesson will have it taught to them by their competitors or their shareholders.

Your willingness to consider your personal future as self-managed rather than system-managed is a requirement of our new economy. The faster you accept this responsibility, the more you can do to make the most of your best, to focus your talents in new ways, and to build your own future.

JOB GROWTH USA

Today's job market is expanding with opportunity. Over 2 million jobs were added to the U.S. economy in the eighteen months ending January 1995. That's almost 30,000 new jobs every working week! Our new productivity as well as our focus on customers and quality is generating more opportunities than anywhere else in the world.

These jobs are not just low-wage service positions. Many have been created to tackle new needs or innovations. Different skills are combined in new ways. The way to keep your earnings up, to become more *employable*, is to acquire and improve the new skills employers are seeking.

Test this for yourself. Think of a job that didn't exist five years ago. Name it.

EMPLOYABILITY

Employability and marketability are the keys to your future. *Employability* is a measure of your *ability to add value* to products and/or situations for the benefit of an organization's established and potential customers. High employability means that you are considered likely to generate measurable results in satisfying the needs of a particular job or department. High employability is probably as close as a person can get to *real job security* these days.

Some American Work Trends

- More than ever before, Americans are building their own small businesses, upgrading or changing their lists of skills, and going back to school.

- The American Association of Retired Persons claims that more people over fifty are leaving their old jobs in large companies and entering the workforce in new ways. These people are no longer retiring to the back porch or the golf links, but are taking on part-time work and medium-term contracts as freelance managers.

- Worldwide competition is stimulating higher standards for product quality, innovation, and diversity. American job seekers are getting the message and learning how to think cross-culturally.

- Because of the explosion in the use of personal computers and information networks and in the fluidity of American work styles, we are strongly positioned for the transition to the Information Age, in which transactions are no longer face-to-face, but terminal-to-terminal, network-to-network. For many, the locus for getting the job done has moved from the formal office to the home, car, ski lodge, or community. People with computer skills have significantly better job prospects than those without. Many are now doing business on the Internet. One of the Baby Bell companies announced it will be publishing a yellow pages business listing for World Wide Web page addresses.

- Reengineering is both loved and hated. It means more than moving the furniture around one more time. Every function and process is reexamined in light of customers' needs. Sacred cows are killed, whole departments are disbanded. Technology replaces workers. People are stretched to learn how to do more and better with less. Mistakes are made, feelings are hurt. The companies that stay committed make it. The others don't.

When employers or potential employers think of you in terms of the value you add rather than the cost you add, they are on the right track. Are you ready to accept your value and commit to developing and promoting it?

Employability is based on competence—*your know-how*. By increasing your skills, you increase your know-how and your employability. The broader your capability, the more employable you are. You can be flexible in assignments, fulfill a range of needs, and take advantage of a variety of opportunities. *Continuous learning* builds employability.

MARKETABILITY

Marketability is a measure of your *ability to communicate* the results you can deliver. If you are very competent and don't know how to tell potential employers what you can do, you will lose opportunities to other candidates.

ACTION PLAN

Nothing happens without action. Read over the material in this part and decide on several action steps you would be willing to take to help gain a new perspective on yourself, your employability, and your future.

ACTIONS TO TAKE   BY WHEN

_____   _____

_____   _____

_____   _____

_____   _____

Take Charge of Your Worklife

You are in charge of your future worklife. Now is the time to understand this and begin to take action. Failure to begin this process weakens your potential for success in the upcoming years.

STEPPING OFF THE TRAIN

In the old view of careers you put your future on track. You boarded a train with a series of known destinations before you. Admittedly, this approach was comfortable and secure. Some career trains were faster than others, some took interesting detours, and some simply made a one-way trip to the end of the line.

The era of career tracks is over. People trying to hold on to their seats may find themselves left at the station, abandoned and going nowhere.

Today, job futures that hold any promise or meaning are self-propelled, multidirectional, and likely to pass through previously uncharted territories. To build the future worklife you want, you will need to get off the train and empower your own movement into lifelong employability.

Questions

Looking back over your past work, how would you describe the track you have been on?

_____

_____

If you were to stay on this track, where would it take you?

_____

_____

RESPONSIBILITY

Like it or not, you are the one person directly responsible for what actually happens in your life—present and future. This means that no matter how you are tempted, you cannot rely on anyone else to make things happen for you. Four or five years from now, when you take stock of how much of your vision has been accomplished, you will see that it has primarily been your own decisions, actions, and readiness to change that have made for your success.

Taking responsibility means simply that you become the *prime mover* in what happens to you. Although there will always be outside circumstances influencing you, it is your response to these circumstances that makes the difference in how everything works out.

Taking responsibility requires these steps:

1. Tell the truth about yourself: facts, attitude, feelings.
2. Eliminate blame and resentment from your conversations.
3. Determine what outcomes you want next and which ones you are willing to work for.
4. Take action toward these outcomes.
5. Observe and assess what results are produced.
6. Go back to step 3 and repeat the process.

THE SELF-DIRECTED EMPLOYEE

As organizations today undergo major change, they respond favorably to employees who take initiative on the job. Although not all managers and supervisors are willing to relinquish control over people in their departments, the true leaders are the first to let go of the old stranglehold.

Leadership in a quality organization means looking for ways to empower people to participate more, to make decisions, and to help increase the overall capacity to serve customers.

Self-directed employees recognize opportunities for increased initiative. They assertively seek to develop their employability and marketability both within and outside the company.

Stop, Look, Listen . . . Then Act

Even in jobs that seem secure, self-directed employees do not become complacent or overly comfortable. It is necessary periodically to *stop* and assess what is happening within the job and within the company; to *look* at how the company is organizing and reorganizing itself; and to *listen* to what the organization's leaders are saying.

Confirm facts, consider a variety of points of view, and then *act*. If there is discussion about a new technology, find someone who understands it *and* can explain it to you. Don't procrastinate.

Keep your sights on the whole job market. If you have left a large organization, resize your thinking to smaller companies. If you are employed within a fairly sizable company, stay in touch with other departments, other company locations, as well as vendors and consultants for your company.

THE FIVE RULES OF HIGH EMPLOYABILITY

Whether you are seeking new work from an employed or unemployed status, the following five areas need your attention.

1. Personal Vision

Know what you want for your future. Translate your vision into opportunities for new life direction, new skills, new jobs or work assignments. Take the first steps to your future.

2. Skills and Capabilities

Know your capabilities. Your skills, competencies, and capabilities are the currency of your future. With the right skills, you are valuable. Without good skills relevant to future needs, you risk your employability and your marketability. When your vision is clear, you must commit to learning the skills and developing the capabilities to fulfill your vision and make it real.

3. Customer Focus

Know your customer(s), including potential employers. Also know your customer's customer, and how products, services, and value flow all the way down the line of customers to the final consumer. If you are not in close two-way communication with those on the customer chain and not continuously on the lookout for better and more efficient ways to improve the value of what you provide, your employability is jeopardized.

4. High Performance

Reach for high performance standards. Your performance is the measurable value you add to any workforce. If you are delivering measurable value significantly greater than what it would cost to employ you, you are more likely to be rewarded with opportunity. If you neglect your performance or let it slip, you may be risking your job. If you have neglected past performance, it may already have cost you your previous job. Seek feedback on your performance, even from past employers.

5. Self-Direction

You must take action to have what you want in your future. Knowing what to do is only the first step; the payoff comes when you're acting on that knowledge. You are the director of your future. You set the direction and you take it.

Even when you know what you want and what you need to do, you will assuredly run into obstacles, barriers, walls, and blocks. Being self-directed means you accept that it may not be easy to build your future the way you want it, but your commitment will not waiver.

Which of these five employability rules do you most need to work on?

_____

_____

_____

Turn to pages 47–52 and complete the Five Rules of High Employability worksheets. These particular worksheets are directed mainly to people who are still employed but feel their current job may be at risk. When done, go on to the next pages.

BARRIERS AND ROADBLOCKS

Every time we commit to produce something worthwhile in our lives, we are guaranteed to hit resistance—sometimes from the outside, sometimes from within. If we weren't going after something, then there wouldn't be resistance. When we become aware of our areas of resistance, we can plan ways to counter them.

In the following list check all barriers or difficulties that could *possibly* inhibit you from accomplishing your most important goals.

- laziness
- tired of working
- procrastination
- fear of failure or rejection
- not knowing what I want
- poor health

- lack of confidence
- not knowing where to look
- personal/family problems
- not willing to take risks
- limited experience in other fields
- nervousness
- money concerns
- fear of change
- anger/resentment
- not good at interviewing
- lack of jobs
- skills out of date

Other personal barriers:

_____

_____

_____

Put a second check next to those that are your most difficult barriers.

Confronting Barriers

Once you have determined which personal barriers are most likely to inhibit your action, then you can gather your resources to bear against it. Discuss the barrier with friends or family. Keep note of the times it gets in your way. Don't blame or criticize yourself for your resistance. Note it, and be willing to act anyway.

Support System

Name four people you can talk with who can willingly provide support if you need it:

_____

_____

_____

_____

ACTION PLAN

Nothing happens without action.

Review the items checked on the previous pages. Then list all of the actions you will take related to the ideas and processes suggested so far to enhance your success at making your future the way you want it to be.

ACTIONS TO TAKE   BY WHEN

_____   _____

_____   _____

_____   _____

_____   _____

_____   _____

Describing Capability

Your employability is your ability to add value to any job situation. Your skills are the ingredients of this value. For example, if you are good at negotiating, your skill might be appealing to a department bargaining with suppliers. If you are computer literate, you may be valuable to a work group using technology to solve its business problems.

Every skill you have makes you *potentially* more valuable to prospective employers within or outside the company. Your future worklife depends on the skills you have to offer.

NOT YOUR JOB TITLE

Do not let your job title define you. **You are not your job title!** You have skills, qualities, and potential that go far beyond the limits of a title. Your job may tap only one or two aspects of what you can do and who you really are. Once you stop taking titles so literally, you will see that you have many "building blocks" that can be reassembled into different profiles for different jobs and work directions, including those so new they're not yet defined by a title.

ADVANCE WORD ABOUT RESUMES

There are a number of resume formats, each requiring some combination of the following components.

- Simple description of past jobs and education
- A targeted work direction or job assignment
- A description of your capabilities, described directly, or implied
- A description of your accomplishments, specific outcomes, or results

INVENTORY YOUR SKILLS

Turn to the worksheets on pages 53–64 and complete the inventories for Describing Capability. Return here.

CAPABILITY REVIEW

Review your Skills for Earning and Qualities for Leadership inventories generated on the worksheets in Section Two. Make sure you didn't leave off any items that could increase your employability, even if they weren't on any of the suggestions lists. Answer the following questions after you have reviewed your work.

1. What skills are most relevant to your current or most recent job?

_____

_____

2. What personal qualities do you think are most important in serving customers?

_____

_____

3. What skills can you translate to other organizations?

_____

_____

4. What personal or leadership qualities are most relevant to your future career growth?

_____

_____

Go back over the above-listed skills and qualities and select the ones that you estimate are the most important to communicate to others.

_____

_____

_____

REALITY TEST

Ask for feedback from a support group, associates, or supervisors about what they see as your best skills and qualities. If you are willing, show your skills and qualities inventories to someone else and ask what they agree with, and what they think you might have forgotten. Look for honest feedback.

INCLUDE YOUR INTERESTS

People spend 10,000 days working during the most productive and active years of their lives. It is essential to your sanity and overall well-being that in some way your personal interests be utilized in the jobs you seek and hold.

In the process of changing jobs, it is easy to panic and just grab the first job offer. However, if you can hold out for work that taps into your personal interests, as well as utilizes your problem-solving skills, the quality of your life will leap forward. Furthermore, when you can integrate your personal motivations and interests with your skills, work is more efficient and even more fun.

Interest Inventory

Your ideal future will combine your skills *and* your personal interests and pleasures.

Check all the items in the list below that represent some of the things you like to do, even if you've never done it, or you don't yet see a connection to your future. Then select from the list your top five interests.

- operate my own business
- work with machinery
- make a good bargain
- do research
- work alone
- attend meetings
- sing or act
- design physical structures
- take care of people
- teach
- travel
- read
- entertain
- advise
- do routine tasks
- work in politics

- work for my community
- sell
- repair things
- manage a task force
- work on a team
- participate in sports
- work with computers
- write
- do physical labor
- negotiate
- serve people
- learn new things
- work in an office
- work outdoors
- dress casually
- have regular hours

- garden
- promote and publicize
- work with numbers
- work for a small firm
- work irregular hours
- work with a large company
- work with technology
- make decisions

- solve problems
- organize work systems
- organize events
- work with my hands
- work with photography
- invent and design
- communicate
- play music

Other things you enjoy:

_____

_____

PERSONAL MOTIVATIONS

The personal motivations and rewards you seek are important to both the quality and the effectiveness of your worklife. Check all of those that are important to you. There will likely be some overlap with your interests.

- financial rewards
- security
- professional advancement
- be in a large organization
- be in a small organization
- work as a consultant
- have clearly defined duties
- work in my home
- work near my home
- be paid on an incentive basis—related to results
- be in charge
- take on projects that haven't been done before
- start my own business
- meet new people
- be challenged
- work closely with others
- be acknowledged for what I accomplish
- manage my own time
- work in attractive surroundings
- be able to "leave the job behind" when I go home
- work directly with clients and customers
- learn/try new things
- use my intelligence
- make my own schedule

get feedback
use my imagination
work in my community
help others

Other personal motivations:

_____

_____

LEARN OR DIE

Perhaps your greatest support in taking charge of your worklife is your willingness to continue your learning and education. This is essential in any worthwhile push to increase your employability and future success. An openness to learning new skills is an asset. Once you have determined what skills you will need for a given job, it is advisable to meet with a career professional, or a person in the field or job in which you are interested, to help you plan on how to acquire these skills.

There are dozens of formal and informal ways to improve your skills. If you have been away from school for a while, it may be frightening to think about returning. Seek sources of encouragement and support. The payoffs for furthering your education are well worth the trouble. In fact, those unwilling to learn will fade from competition. The underlying message is: Learn or Die.

If you are interested in a major job or career change, you should plan for the long term: perhaps over four to five years.

ACTION PLAN . . . GOALS FOR LEARNING

Review the Goals for Learning worksheets on pages 61–64. What are the most immediate steps you will take to increase your learning or development?

ACTIONS TO TAKE   BY WHEN

_____   _____

_____   _____

Describing Results

The most direct way to become known as valuable to a potential employer is to effectively describe your results. Unless you can write and speak powerfully about yourself, there is little chance that anyone will know your worth. Personal marketability comes through strategic and effective communications—written and verbal.

This marketability starts with the skills and qualities inventories in the Describing Capability worksheets, lists of accomplishments from the Describing Results worksheets, and a variety of resumes that can be custom-tailored to your needs. In the Writing Letters section you will put together strategic letters to obtain interviews and to follow up on employment opportunities.

Tip: When you complete the material in this and the upcoming pages that defines and describes your skills and strengths, practice putting the written words into real conversation with role plays and other interactions—perhaps with a counselor or coach—to get in the habit of selling yourself.

ACCOMPLISHMENTS

An accomplishment is a result you have produced. An accomplishment is something tangible that gives a potential employer the assurance that your capabilities and qualities will generate predictable outcomes. The more accomplishments you can communicate, the easier it is to market yourself.

It is important to make the distinction between *results* and *activities*. An *activity* is what you do or did: "Organized people to work together." A *result* is what the effort produced: "Built a team that reduced process time by 40%." A result is what generates the payoff or value added.

Activity: Headed a major reengineering project.
Result: Decreased the number of transactions by 50%.

Activity: Planned and implemented a new coding system.
Result: Reduced error rate to beat industry standards.

Activity: Initiated a quality improvement process.
Result: Quality improved dramatically in 90 days.

In the past people mostly described themselves from their job titles or responsibilities: "I was responsible for scheduling training sessions." Responsibilities usually describe duties, not results. Today, job descriptions are becoming obsolete. In this section and on the worksheets associated with it, you will be building an inventory of accomplishments to use in your resumes and to describe in interviews.

Quick Pass

Answer the following questions. Be sure to use the language of results.

What is a result you produced at home you are proud of?

_____

_____

_____

What is another result from your personal life that you are proud of?

_____

_____

_____

What is something you accomplished in school?

_____

_____

_____

What are you proud of in earlier work?

_____

_____

_____

What is a recent accomplishment?

_____

_____

_____

What have you accomplished related to personal development and learning?

_____

_____

_____

INVENTORY YOUR ACCOMPLISHMENTS

Turn to the worksheets on pages 65–68 and complete the inventories for Describing Results. Then record the key actions you will take to build your skills.

ACTION PLAN

Nothing happens without action.

Review the material from pages 36–37 and on the worksheets pages 93–99. List three people you should communicate to about your strengths and accomplishments. This could include current or past supervisors, current or past colleagues, counselors, or family.

1. Communicate about: _____

To: _____

By (date) _____

2. Communicate about: _____

To: _____

By (date) _____

3. Communicate about: _____

To: _____

By (date) _____

A RESUME TUTORIAL

Note: Review this material in advance of starting your resume. Then have it available when you are doing your actual resumes on the worksheets.

What Makes a Good Resume?

A good resume is a self-marketing tool for finding a job or for making a career change. It is a well-structured, easy-to-read presentation of your work history, skills, and results, designed to convince a potential employer to invite you to an interview.

Your resume should have the same impact on a reader as any good product print ad. Enhanced by powerful language, all successful print ads give their readers the facts about a product's performance and effectiveness. A really good resume will convey the same kind of message about you.

The best resume writers focus their presentation on a targeted job or skill area, whether or not this is ever explicitly stated. By having a specific job target in view, a good resume will focus those things about you that are most relevant to the position or work assignment you seek. The era of "one size fits all" resumes is long over. Computer software allows you to adapt each resume quickly to a particular situation for maximum impact.

Power Language

In your resume you use language that makes you most attractive to the potential hirer. Hopefully, you have already built a good set of skills and accomplishments in previous parts of this book. You can put these to use in organizing powerful resumes.

Here are some examples of powerful phrases drawn from successful current resumes:

- To move swiftly and capably from task to task, from one work environment to another, from soft product to hard product, and even across national boundaries
- To master new concepts, skills, and practices
- To be versatile, flexible, and mobile
- To learn quickly, adapt to change, and engage innovatively in problem solving

- To organize and reorganize new data, work systems, and corporate processes, according to evolving needs
- To integrate and balance diverse functions
- To be entrepreneurial, but risk-smart
- To focus on customer needs
- To work comfortably with diversity
- To use computer technology, including the Internet and the World Wide Web
- To engage with networks of people and information
- To work on special task forces and project teams
- To be quality-oriented
- To think multinationally

Take a few moments to review the above list, and check or circle those statements that could relate to you.

RESUME PREPARATION GUIDELINES

- Always prepare your resume with a targeted job or assignment in mind, even if you do not specifically state it. This will help you determine what to include or leave out.
- Use short indented phrases where appropriate—with a bullet (•) or an asterisk (*) before each—rather than complete sentences. See samples.
- Choose the clearest, simplest language to say what you want to say. Even in the same industry, outsiders frequently won't understand your company lingo.
- Use specific quantities, percentages, or dollar values where they enhance your description of a result.
- Put the strongest statements at the top of each section or paragraph.
- Do not use "I." It is implied throughout.
- Do not include hobbies, vocational or social interests unless they clearly demonstrate or contribute to your ability to perform the targeted job or assignment.
- Avoid gratuitous self-descriptions, such as "Seasoned self-starter."
- Describe results and achievements, such as "Completed three major research projects on time and within budget."
- Have someone with good language skills check for spelling, punctuation, and grammar.

Where possible, statements on your resume should describe all of the following:

- The activity: "Coordinated auditing reports"
- The person/department/company for whom the activity was performed: "for the compliance division"

- The results of that activity performed for that person/department or division: "allowing 48-hour turnarounds"

Length

Keep it short and simple. If well written and edited, a one-page resume is frequently sufficient to describe your best capabilities. As with really good print ads, less is more. A second resume page is suggested only if you have a lengthy career history in which each transition is very important, or if your work involved a number of recognizable products. It is also acceptable if you have written for a variety of publications, received a series of honors or awards, or obtained a number of patents, and these additional details would encourage a potential employer to want to meet you.

Resume Don'ts

- Don't include a photograph.
- Don't list references or that they are "available upon request."
- Don't enclose your resume in a binder or folder.
- Don't list gender, weight, state of health, or other extraneous personal data.
- Don't include mailing address of prior employers (city and state are sufficient).

Formats

There are three standard formats and one new "internal" format suggested:

Chronological
Functional
Targeted
Capabilities Resume—Internal

Each format serves different needs. In the Resume Catalog (Section Three), we also include customized examples to show how the three standard formats are modified for recent graduates and for people who are self-employed or working as independent consultants.

WRITING YOUR RESUME

Your first step is to decide on the resume format that will support your employment strategy. Review the material on the upcoming pages to decide upon the best format, then use the format guide in the worksheets to help confirm your decision.

Once you have decided on the format to follow, go to the Resume Details section related to that resume format (pages 25–31) and follow this when you are assembling your resume. You can also go to Section Three, Resume Catalog, page 115, where we provide a large variety of sample resumes. These are our suggestions. You, of course, are the responsible party, so you may change the rules if you wish.

To prepare your resume, you need to have completed the worksheets on Describing Capability and Describing Results. These worksheets are on pages 53–69. After you have decided on the format that supports your employment strategy (see page 81 for help), and read the relevant material on that format on the upcoming pages, turn to the Writing Resumes worksheets on pages 81–92 and draft your resume in pencil. Later you will need to input this on a word processor.

Resume Details

THE CHRONOLOGICAL RESUME

The chronological resume highlights a good work history that relates directly to your next targeted job. There should be no major time gaps and few employer changes within your work history.

1. Start with your present or most recent position and work backward in time, devoting the most space to your most recent employment.
2. Detail only the last eight to ten years or three or four positions you held. Summarize previous positions simply and briefly, even if they are relevant to your present targeted work. One-line descriptions are sufficient and could be put under a heading "Other Relevant Experience."
3. For experience with different employers, cite years, not months and days, on your job history. You can provide exact detail on an application.
4. It's not necessary to list every change of position within a given employer. List those that are relevant to your next targeted job. Be sure to list your most recent positions.
5. Do not repeat details common to several positions.
6. For each position, include the major results that demonstrate your competency on that job. Secondary results and achievements can be left off if you have already been clear about your major accomplishments.
7. Always keep your targeted work in mind, emphasizing only those past jobs and results that are most closely related.
8. If you have earned a formal degree within the past two years and have less than two years of work history, list your degree at the top of your resume. See the New or Recent Graduates section in the Resume Catalog. Otherwise, education should be the last-listed item on your resume.
9. Keep the language clear and crisp. Keep it short.

Sample Chronological Resume

RICHARD ARMIGER
114 Ralston Road
Richmond, VA 23235
(804) 555-6643

1994 - 1996   Century Corporate Towers   Richmond, VA
BUILDING MANAGER

Managed two 12-story twin corporate towers from early construction through completion totaling 700,000 s.f. Directed activities for all areas:

- Operated heating, ventilation, and air conditioning.
- Supervised custodial services including marble restoration.
- Coordinated corporate tenant relocation, completion of tenant suites and additional construction needs.
- Assigned maintenance personnel for building needs.
- Supervised maintenance of two six-level parking garages, corporate park roadways and all entrances.
- Managed fire detection, emergency generators, security access, elevator systems, inside and outside decorative pools and general ambiance.

1964 - 1994   Richmond Police Department   Richmond, VA

1986 - 1994   LIEUTENANT

- Supervised maintenance of Richmond Police Station.
- Prepared budget requests for Support Services Division.
- Directed the installation of traffic signs, signals, and road markings.
- Purchased and replaced police cruisers and oversaw entire fleet maintenance.
- Managed personnel in Support Services Division.
- Created computer programs for burglar alarms, accident data, and vehicle preventive maintenance systems.

1979 - 1986   SERGEANT

1974 - 1979   DETECTIVE

1964 - 1974   PATROL OFFICER

EDUCATION

1980   University of Richmond
A.S. - Criminal Justice

Graduate, FBI Academy: Quantico, VA

THE FUNCTIONAL RESUME

The functional resume features skill areas grouped together according to their relationship to your targeted job. In a functional resume, you can focus the reader's attention on selected functional or skill areas while minimizing any gaps or inconsistencies in your work history. If you're changing jobs or work direction, or newly entering or reentering the job market, the functional resume will allow you to include nonpaid work experiences, like school, community, or volunteer activities.

1. Use two to four separate categories or sections, each one highlighting a particular area of skill or results, such as: Administration, Field Repair, Counseling, Supervision.
2. List these functional categories in order of importance to your targeted job, with the most relevant category at the top. This first paragraph usually contains the most information as well.
3. Within each category, stress those results that most directly relate to your targeted work. These need not necessarily relate to a previous employment situation.
4. Again, formal education is listed at the bottom of the resume, unless you have earned a formal degree within the past two years and you have fewer than two years of work history. If your degree is in a field completely unrelated to your targeted job, list it at the very end, no matter how recently it was received.
5. List your job history in the last third of the resume, giving dates, employers, and job titles.
6. Keep the resume length to one page whenever possible. See page 23 for exceptions.

Sample Functional Resume

GINA CRISPOR
323 West End Avenue
New York, NY 10023
(212) 555-6651 AOL@CRISPO

WRITING / FREELANCE

- Wrote twelve-article series on personal development, fashion, and home furnishings for *Co-Ed* magazine.
- Wrote feature articles for *Ingenue* magazine.
- Created home-sewing shows for *Co-Ed*, given in major department stores nationwide.
- Co-authored paperback book on teenage problems for Pen Publications.

FILMSTRIP PRODUCTION

- Produced "Loving Relationships"- a half-hour filmstrip for high school students for *Co-Ed*. Wrote "Beautiful Foods" filmstrip for *Co-Ed* magazine.
- Edited over 50 filmstrips for use by high schools in areas of music, art history, and literature for Bramston Publications.

FUND RAISING

- Assumed major responsibilities in scholarship fundraising efforts, reaching goals up to $130,000.
- Created craft projects and directed weekly workshops, which produced hundreds of items for large handicrafts bazaar.
- Organized theatrical and cultural benefits, bringing in over $48,000 in three years.

WORK HISTORY

1990 - Present   **Freelance Writer and Fund-Raiser**

1988 - 1990   PARAMETER PUBLICATIONS: New York, NY

                      Editor, *Ideas For Youth:* Wrote articles and supervised art.

1984 - 1988   *CO-ED MAGAZINE*: New York, NY

                      Fashion Editor: Covered fashion markets; supervised photography, art, layout, wrote copy; produced fashion show. Received editorial excellence award from Institute of Men's and Boy's Wear.

EDUCATION

1984   U.C.L.A.
               B.A. - Art History/English

THE TARGETED RESUME

Unlike the chronological and functional resumes, which describe results you have delivered or produced, the targeted resume includes what you can or *could* do—looking forward—to fulfill or even exceed the requirements of your targeted job. Use the targeted format when you are very clear about a particular job or work assignment you want. In this format it is customary to create numerous resumes, customizing them for specific employers and their individual requirements.

The more you know about your targeted job or work, the easier it will be to select the related capabilities and accomplishments. Only those capabilities and accomplishments directly or indirectly related to your targeted job should be listed. A targeted resume is very easy to read. Everything is straightforward.

1. Describe your targeted job or work at the top of the resume right under your name and address. You can either name a particular title or describe a function, such as Data Programming Consultant or Service Coordination for Earthmoving Equipment.
2. Keep your statements of capabilities and accomplishments short—one or two lines.
3. The skills or capabilities you list should answer the question "What can you do for me (my company or work group)?"
4. The accomplishments or results you list should answer the question "What have you done to demonstrate that you can do what you say?"
5. Work history and education are described on the bottom third of the resume.

STEPHEN HAWKE
3 Dalton Place
Dallas, TX 75265
(214) 555-9008 fax - (214) 555-9779

JOB TARGET   RECRUITMENT CONSULTING/STAFF DEVELOPMENT

CAPABILITIES

- Utilize expertise in organizational development and management, including strategic planning, decision making, problem solving, and creating organizational structure.
- Generate unity of purpose and energy to achieve goals.
- Manage total operations and logistics, including fiscal, administrative, and labor force.
- Coordinate instructional programs, including program planning, instructor training, and delivery.

ACCOMPLISHMENTS

- Directed largest recruiting station in Air Force with a staff of 132 and $1.3 million operational budget. Oversaw 42 subfacilities in a three-state area. Managed contracting, vendor services, and facilities.
- Procured 7.5% of total Air Force recruitment, regularly surpassing recruitment goals. Developed successful marketing plan, achieving 37% market share.
- Developed Air Force Recruitment Training Program from ground up, including program design, instructor training, and quality control. Increased enrollment from 3,000 to 15,000 in one year.
- Implemented systems, staff assignments, and management practices of educational training facilities to withstand 60% annual turnover in personnel.

WORK HISTORY

1990 - 1996   U.S. AIR FORCE RECRUITING STATION: Dallas, TX
Executive Officer

1983 - 1990   U.S. AIR FORCE SCHOOLS: Colorado Springs, CO
Director of Educational Services

EDUCATION

1988   MANAGEMENT SCHOOL: U.S.A.F. - Colorado Springs, CO

1986   COMMAND/STAFF COLLEGE: U.S.A.F. - Colorado Springs, CO

1982   UNIVERSITY of TEXAS, Austin, TX
B.A.

THE CAPABILITIES RESUME—INTERNAL

Answering the call for the new self-directed employee is the capabilities resume—internal. This format attempts to translate someone's core competencies, star qualities, and skills or capabilities within an organization to facilitate his or her obtaining interviews for internal transfer or reassignment. Similar to the targeted resume, the capabilities resume requires research from the individual employee as well as a spirit of initiative.

Use the capabilities format when you are very clear about a particular job or work assignment you want within your existing organization. In this format you can create numerous resumes, customizing them for specific departments or work areas and their individual requirements.

The more you know about your desired work assignment or internal transfer, the easier it will be to formulate the introductory cover statement as well as the related capabilities and accomplishments. Only those capabilities and accomplishments directly or indirectly related to your desired assignment should be listed. A capabilities resume is very brief and easy to read. The overall focus should keep it clear and unambiguous.

1. In the introductory cover statement, which is like a mini cover letter, briefly describe your understanding of a perceived or well-known need, as well as your specific ability to meet that need. For example: "With the latest upheavals in the Marketing and Customer Services Division, the needs for employee retraining are becoming obscured by well-meaning attempts to keep everyone from panic. My writing skills, as well as my coaching and facilitation capability, might be helpful to you at this time."
2. Keep your statements of capabilities and accomplishments short—one or two lines.
3. The skills or capabilities you list should answer the question "What capability do you have to back up your introductory statement?"
4. The accomplishments or results you list should answer the question "Can you furnish factual backup to demonstrate your capabilities in action?"
5. Recent employment history within your company and very recent education/training are listed last.
6. This resume is best kept to one page. A note at the bottom tells the reader you're attaching a standard resume (it will help) to add some detail about your overall capability. If you wish, you may substitute the attached standard resume with other supporting information, such as awards, affiliations, or even nonwork accomplishments.

Sample Capabilities Resume—Internal

JAN 12, 1997

TO: **FRANCES COSGROVE**   Group Leader - Systems Projects
Systems and Technology Business   555-1515, ext. 79

FROM: **RICH LANGSTON,**   Product Planner/Market Analyst
Product Planning/Market Support Division   555-1414, ext. 61

INTRODUCTION:

I understand the S. & T. business will be breaking into five distinct smaller groups and that product research and marketing will dovetail with specific systems I'm familiar with. I have strong skills in planning, negotiating, programming and presenting, as well as in leading initiatives. I believe I belong with you on a first rate team.

CAPABILITIES: Some of my capabilities / core competencies are:

- Being a teacher and a coach, with strong interpersonal skills.
- Contributing as an individual or as a project leader.
- Technical writing - knowledge of Bookmaster, Process Master, XEDIT.
- Results-oriented, focusing on technical and logistical support.
- Analytical; study statistics and translate complex systems outputs to customers.

ACCOMPLISHMENTS: A partial list of my demonstrated results:

- Acted as liaison worldwide with seven foreign divisions to support technical translations for every level of customer.
- Coordinated the design and writing of marketing flyers reaching 35,000 customers in 17 countries.
- Taught TSO to scores of new programmers in the IS division of HP.
- Wrote 90-page program operation manual for internal HP cost accounting system.

RECENT HEWLETT-PACKARD HISTORY:

Product Planning/Market Support Coordinator Product Planning/Market Support Division	1995-present
Technical Writer/Systems Assurance Programmer Development, Applications and Systems Division	1992-1995
Information Systems Programmer, Teacher Information Systems Division	1990-1992

RECENT TRAINING / DEVELOPMENT:

WWW page design and high speed access transfers	1996-present

Previous work history, education/training: see attached standard resume.

DRAFT YOUR RESUME

You should have a different version of your resume for each function or job you have targeted. If you're considering two or three jobs in the same general field and you are using either the chronological or the functional resume format, then one version will do. If your targeted jobs are functionally different from each other, then you will need a different version of your resume for each.

COMPUTING YOUR FUTURE

Having data-based software to generate resumes offers advantages previously unavailable. What are they?

- By keeping a stockpile of powerful skills and accomplishments on disk, you can cut and paste them in a variety of combinations to emphasize specific skill areas, accomplishments, or capability.
- New skills and results can be added to your database as they're attained.
- You can experiment with a variety of formats, fonts, and styles to come up with just the right resume for any new opportunity.
- Data can be edited to fit one page or two, depending on the requirements.
- Any one paragraph or section can be revised and/or expanded without affecting areas you don't want to change.
- Good resume programs can work with a laser printer for top-quality appearance.

LAYOUT, TYPING, AND TYPOGRAPHY

The visual organization of your resume helps to guide the reader's eye to the most important points and to strengthen the overall presentation. A good layout helps focus the reader's attention. Some elements that contribute to a good layout include:

- UPPERCASE LETTERS: for important headings or titles.
- Underlining: rarely used. However, when used, it can highlight a dramatic statement you don't want the reader to miss. Use sparingly.
- *Italics* and **bold**: currently considered easier on the eye than underlining. Use sparingly.
- Highlighting: a sometimes useful technique. Use a translucent color pen to dramatize key points on the resume for different employers. Use conservatively—it is unconventional.

Good print ad layouts make generous use of empty space on the page, known in the trade as *air* or *white space*. It helps to accent what is on the page in a way that is restful to the eye and mind. Create white space in your resume with wide margins, double-spacing between paragraphs, careful positioning of your name and address, and indentations. Caution: Don't overdo. Refer to Section Three, Resume Catalog.

More Detail

- Make sure your name, address, and phone number are left-justified or centered at the top of your resume.
- Use at least one-inch margins on all sides of the page.
- Allow plenty of white space.
- Bulleted statements are easier to read than paragraphs, although they take up more space on the page.
- Single-space the text of your resume, double-space between paragraphs.

Several Drafts

Don't expect to achieve a finished resume with your first draft. Plan to revise several times. Once you have assembled all pertinent data, edit carefully, cutting back sentences that are too long and eliminating repetitions and unclear language.

Final Critique

Ask someone with good grammar and spelling skills to scan, proofread, and critique your first and second drafts. Don't plan to do this alone. Most of us are blind to our own writing errors.

Make sure you ask your resume critic to be as tough as possible, pointing out any errors and lack of clarity. Avoid discussions of format, content, or emphasis, unless you are consulting a professional in these matters.

CHECKLIST FOR FINAL REVIEW

- The material fits neatly on one or two pages.
- There are no spelling, grammar, or punctuation errors.
- Your name, address, phone, and fax/E-mail numbers are centered or left-justified at the top.
- No paragraphs or sections are longer than eight lines.
- Bold or capital letters are used to emphasize important titles—but not to excess.
- Indentations are used to separate different areas and organize information logically.

- Extraneous personal information (height, weight, age, gender) has been excluded.
- Sentences and paragraphs are edited to eliminate unnecessary or repetitious information.
- The printed page is neat, clean, and professional-looking.
- The overall appearance of the page is attractive to the reader.
- The resume showcases your employability.

PRINTING AND DUPLICATING

Once your resume meets your highest standards, it's time to make copies. If you have a laser printer, you can print individual copies from your own word processor or computer.

If you will be making a number of copies or if you do not have a laser printer available, print master copies of the resume, and get it printed or duplicated at a local quality copy shop. Some shops will be able to take a computer disk as input.

Insist on good-quality paper stock. Pure white is fine, but ivory, buff, or off-white tend to stand out more against the piles of paper that clutter most desks.

Should you make copies on your handy local photocopy machine? Unfortunately, the quality is often not good enough. The image sometimes smears, the paper is usually fairly low-grade, and the printing isn't consistent. Some advanced machines, however, are quite acceptable. You're the judge—go for the best.

Listing Your Contacts and Using Your Networks

In any major change situation it is helpful to enlist everyone and anyone who can assist you in getting what you want. And yet, there is sometimes a natural resistance to turning to others at a time of need. There is a tendency to want to prove yourself, hold on to what's left of your pride, to avoid revealing the need for help.

This is particularly so where the problem might be sensitive, like a job or career change, when you need inside help or information to get beyond overwhelming competition. It is a big mistake to avoid, rather than seek out, people who might have information, contacts, or advice to offer. This avoidance can cost you dearly in the time it takes for you to get "connected" to what you want.

It's wise to be working to develop contacts throughout your active worklife. Who are these contacts? Keep track of as many people as you can who know about the field you are in or the area of work you are targeting. Include people who naturally could know others. By the time you find someone who knows another person, who asks a third person for a lead to someone else, you are starting to build a list of dozens or scores of potential leads. An old saying goes: "Everyone knows someone who knows someone who knows someone. Anyone is within four people of getting to the President or the Pope."

Myths

- That you should not present your troubles to anyone else
- That people are not interested in helping others
- That important people do not return phone calls to strangers
- That it is too late; everyone else must have contacted the person you need to talk to, so why bother
- That you don't know anyone important
- That it is impossible to reach people at work, and you don't want to bother them at home

The organized and aggressive use of personal referral networks is the hallmark of a good job searcher. Networks can be used to acquire contacts, feedback, introductions, coaching, and counseling. Consider networks as sources of information that may lead you to information and contacts—not as sources of jobs themselves.

CATEGORIES

Here are some of the types of people to include in your personal support network:

- Close family: in-laws, cousins, uncles, aunts, brothers, sisters, fiancés, ex-spouses
- Work contacts: colleagues you see day by day (or ex-colleagues you used to see) and those who have retired or transferred; customers, suppliers, consultants, supervisors, managers, directors, board members
- Competitors: people whom you have heard of or met in meetings or conventions, or have been told about by present and past customers
- Professionals: lawyers, bankers, consultants, teachers, government officials
- Authorities: people you have read about or those who have written articles in the field
- Social contacts: people you meet at parties, weddings, wakes, conventions, class reunions; people in chat rooms on the Net

KEEPING TRACK

Just start with the names and note how they might help you. Then we can help you organize these names and put them to work for you.

Go to the Listing Your Contacts and Using Your Networks worksheets on pages 93–99.

Writing Letters with Power

The last step in the entire change process is accomplished through language: phone, mail, cyberspace, person-to-person. The ability to write powerful letters is an essential tool for your work development or job campaign.

COVER LETTERS

Even with highly polished writing and editing, the basic resume can still be a generalized, impersonal communication. Potential employers might have to interpret, analyze, and predict how your skills and capabilities can be put to work for their immediate situation. Sometimes employers interpret well, and sometimes they don't. Once you have produced your best resume, a custom cover letter is your next step to ensure making a direct hit right in the center of the employer's interest.

The purpose of the custom cover letter is to communicate a *specific, personalized* message to a *particular* employer, answering the most fundamental employment question of all: *Why should I hire you?* The cover letter is your way to so distinguish what you have to offer that the likelihood of an interview is greatly enhanced. Given the complexity and competitiveness of today's employment market, the cover letter is an important tool for expanding and increasing employability.

A custom cover letter should accompany every resume you send out. Given the aptitude of word processors and software, this step is easier than ever before. Simply follow some basic rules.

COVER LETTER RULES

Rule 1. Address a Person, Not a Title

Personal letters are read far sooner than form letters. Think of yourself when you open the mail. Letters addressed to you personally are the first read. The form letter to "Sir," "Madam," or "Occupant" may never be read.

Call your targeted companies and ask for the name and title of the person in charge of the function or department where you have a work interest, the person who can make the hiring decision. It may take more than one call. Do not get overwhelmed with explaining that you're looking for job opportunities. Say you have material to send and you want to ensure it gets to the right person.

With a little practice you'll find there isn't much problem in obtaining the names and titles you're seeking. Don't make the mistake of aiming too high. Find a person at the department level—ideally, the person you would work for if you get the job or assignment.

Rule 2. Communicate Something Personal

People who get a lot of mail have understandably developed techniques to skim quickly before reading to see if, in fact, the letter has a message for them. Many employers now use scanners on both resumes and cover letters to simply seek out key words to help them sort through mountains of mail.

In your opening lines, write something that is uniquely associated with the person, department, or organization and that will show the reader you invested the time to investigate them as your customer. Some typical personal openings:

> *I see that you have opened a new shopping mall on the western side of town.*

> *Daria Foster in the economics department mentioned your role in the university's expansion plans.*

> *I understand that you have just received a new government contract for telecommunications relays.*

Rule 3. Answer the Question "Why should I see you?"

The work world operates on *value*, not need. You are as interesting to potential employers as their perception of *your value to them*.

In the body of your cover letter communicate some special way that your skills will be valuable to the potential employer. First, demonstrate your interest in the employer as your customer. Then tell the employer how you perceive that your skills might meet their needs. This will take some basic research in your target field and familiarity with the interests and needs of the specific employer, plus a willingness to show how you can make a difference. Common sense helps, as the following examples indicate.

I feel that my organizational skills could help you in setting up your new customer service department. As you can see from my resume, I have experience in handling service calls in a related field and, as I have already been through several years of reengineering, I could help your staff understand and work through this transition.

I know you are aware of the need for good publicity and effective grassroots outreach within your local community. My skills in this area in my own suburban community could assist you in getting the exposure you want.

Take some risks in describing what you feel you can do for a potential employer. Even if you're somewhat off target, the fact that you are addressing their needs with your value (skills/capabilities/competencies) will create interest. A well-thought-out, well-written cover letter demonstrates your individual proactivity. You took the time to attend to the potential employer as your own customer.

In focusing on the needs in an organization, beware of writing in critical overtones. Never put down the efforts a company has already initiated, no matter what you really think. Simply communicate your ability to assist, enhance, and support.

Rule 4. Speak Their Language

Every field has its own jargon and technology. Use the right terms to indicate your ability and expertise. An excellent way to improve your knowledge of the language of any field is to read trade journals and articles by professionals in that particular field. See your librarian. Use the electronic bulletin board.

Rule 5. Ask for the Interview

This is called the "close"—the time when you ask for the business. In this case the "business" is a personal *meeting*—a more subtle word than "interview." Ask for it. You can even suggest a date and time. Here are some sample closings:

I'm planning to schedule interviews in the Phoenix area for next month and would like to meet with you during the first week of May. I will call you to set up a possible date.

I will be in your area on other business on the 16th of this month and would like to see you then if it's convenient.

SAMPLE COVER LETTER

The cover letter and the interview follow-up letter are most important in the change process. Sample sentences and phrases are provided in the worksheets on pages 108–14. The following is a successful cover letter.

12268 Mountain Lane
Denver, CO 80204
January 17, 1997

Ms. Susan Jones
Assistant Manager
Computer World
134 Beacon Street
Boston, MA 02478

Dear Ms. Jones:

I saw your notice in the *Denver Post* about the customer service position for Computer World. The qualities you need are a close match to the ones I've developed. I have four years of experience with computer systems, and I'm sure my skills might be useful to you right away.

I know that a successful service representative has to take care of customers in a way that is helpful and efficient. These are characteristics that I've developed in organizing and presiding over our county's computer users' group. Members in this group must thoroughly know DOS, Windows and Windows 95, and Macintosh computer environments, and provide service to other people in the community. Last year we served over five hundred individuals and consistently received high ratings on the quality of our services from our clients.

I am confident my knowledge and abilities will be of value to Computer World. I would like a few minutes of your time to discuss my qualifications. I will contact you next Friday to arrange a meeting. If you have any questions in the meantime, please call.

Best regards,

Leroy Alexander
303-555-5678

You, the Entrepreneur

An entrepreneur is a person who takes the risk for the success of a new business idea.

All jobs in today's market are entrepreneurial, in that you are more than ever before at risk for your results. You are asked to be responsible for tangible outcomes almost as if your job were a separate little business. Some people are successfully making transitions from regular jobs to small businesses or consultancies—often with their former employer as the client. More than 75 percent of new jobs added to the economy in the past ten years have come from small start-up businesses. New organizations are starting every day to fill the ever-changing needs of customers for new services and products. Entrepreneurs recognize what's needed and wanted in their communities and provide service in these areas. Opportunities abound: home crafts, mail order, computer service and repair, counseling and consulting are just a few of the growing areas reachable without large capitalization.

In starting a small business, you must be concerned not only with the ability to solve a problem or deliver a service to a customer but also with the entire system supporting such an endeavor. A businessperson must be engaged in the creative, administrative, financial, and sales and marketing areas as well as in a variety of other details.

STEPS FOR FORMING A SUCCESSFUL SMALL BUSINESS

1. A creative spark lights up an idea that solves a problem or responds to an available opportunity that is valuable to a customer or potential customer.
2. This idea is formulated into a "business proposition" that produces a measurable result—a product or service that can be produced by you (and others).
3. The product or service is tested for customer relevance. Does it mean something to people in practical, realistic, everyday terms?
4. The product or service is repeatable—not just a one-shot deal. The entrepreneur is able to turn it out each and every time.
5. The business or service is economically viable. That is, the business

can grow to the point where the outbound value delivered produces an income greater than the cost of producing that value.

6. The business is replicable. This is the key to expansion. Having been able to demonstrate the economic viability, the owner can actually see the service multiply through others without personally having to do all the work.

7. The business is competitive. Once a business starts to succeed, people notice it, and competition goes up. A good business is able to maintain a competitive edge of quality, innovation, and price.

8. The business is inherently satisfying personally. People in the business feel nurtured to the degree to which they contribute to the business.

9. The business remains true to its purpose. The organization continues to contribute the value originally intended.

Questions

If you decided that you wanted to start your own business, what services or products would you want to provide?

_____

_____

What would make you successful?

_____

_____

DANGER AHEAD FOR A SMALL BUSINESS

Many businesses fail in their first six months, leaving unhappiness and, sometimes, financial distress. Keep your eyes open for some of the following difficulties in a new business.

- Getting most of your advice from friends—who tend to agree—rather than trying the ideas on an independent, impartial evaluator
- Not first testing your ideas on a small scale
- Trying to start too large or grow too fast
- Having a good idea and not the means to make it real
- Spending too long "getting ready," rather than launching the product or service
- Not researching the competition
- Not keeping accurate records (You could run out of money before you know it.)
- Not being open to constructive criticism
- Having your ego too deeply involved

- Borrowing too much money before profits are seen
- Getting in on a "fad" too late
- Not having appropriate professional advice
- Trying to do it all yourself, including areas in which you have no proven competence
- Charging too little or too much for personal services
- Lack of consistency or follow-through
- Accumulating too many creditors
- Not being willing to sell assertively
- Undefined relationships with partners (Put it in writing.)
- Inflexibility and holding on too long to unworkable ideas or ways of working

CHECK YOUR E.Q. (ENTREPRENEURIAL QUOTIENT)

Listed below are personal qualities and attributes characteristic of successful business people or entrepreneurs. Check each quality or characteristic, indicating where you think you stand.

	definitely	frequently	able to develop	average	below average
Innovative					
Goal-oriented					
Realistically optimistic					
Assertive					
Responsive					
Persistent					
Responsible					
Service-oriented					
Respond well to challenge					
Open to feedback					
Able to accept disappointment					
Willing to take risks					

In summary, are you a future entrepreneur?

SECTION TWO

WORKSHEETS

WORKSHEETS

The Five Rules of High Employability

These first sets of worksheets are mainly for those of you still employed and looking to move within your own organization.

Explore ways of increasing your employability and determine actions you can take to drive your future in the direction you want.

1 | PERSONAL VISION

Know what you want for your future:

How clear are you about how you want to be working in your future? Have you identified the ideal jobs (work assignments) for you?

- ▓ I have no idea.
- ▓ I have some ideas.
- ▓ I know the field I want to be in.
- ▓ I have more than two targets for work areas mixing my skills and interests.

Do you know the skills you need to learn to be most employable?

- ▓ Not yet.
- ▓ I have a general idea.
- ▓ I know specifically what I need to learn.
- ▓ I know what I need to learn and how I can learn it.

Check the actions that interest you:

- ▓ Have a sense of your own life's journey and the courage to include it in future work.

- Stay in touch with your own standards of what makes a good life. Don't sacrifice quality of life to standard of living.

- Be willing to reinvent a work direction, to propose a way of working that is different from the way it was previously done.

- Focus on desired future directions you could perform well with some training; then inventory the training needs and go for it.

- Pay attention to jobs outside the company so you can gain perspective on a larger market for your services. Read about other fields, and network with people who can advise you on what is needed in these fields.

- Review media materials/commentaries (newspaper want ads, trade journals, general business publications, TV and radio reports) with an eye to potential job development in areas of interest.

- Use career/job training and other supportive workshops and classes to help formulate your future goals and enhance employability.

- Talk about your job development interests to significant people within the company.

- Participate in personal development courses that can assist you in making career transitions.

2 | SKILLS AND CAPABILITIES

Know your capabilities:

Do you know what your most marketable skills are? Within the company? In the outside world?

- Not very clear.

- I know what I'm best at in the eyes of others.

- I know generally where my skills can be very useful.

- I know several places that would want me working for them.

Do you know how to improve your skills?

- I don't know what I need to learn.

- I know I need some new skills training.

- I have some specific courses in mind.

- I am committed to taking some specific courses.

Check the actions that interest you:

- Complete the Skills for Earning section in this book.

- Seek and obtain honest feedback from peers about your strengths and weaknesses.

- Find out from human resources professionals about the skills and competencies that are thought to be most needed in the future of the company and industry.

- Use corporate training funds (if available) and other supportive workshops and classes to help formulate your future goal and meet developmental needs.

- Focus development not only on hard skills but also on valuable new attitudes and work qualities that are needed: leadership qualities, openness to innovation, communication, team building, and more. Upgrade your E.I.—Emotional Intelligence.

- Prepare a practical set of learning goals using the Goals for Learning section in this book. Share this with people who can help you make it happen.

- Pay attention to skills that you might not use today at work but that could support your move to a new work direction inside or outside the company.

3 | CUSTOMER FOCUS

Know your customer(s), including potential employers:

How well do you know the needs of your customer (potential employer)?

- Unclear who my real customer is.

- I know who my customer is.

- I regularly get feedback from customers.

- I am very close to their needs.

Do you know the improvements your customer(s) wants to see in the work you deliver?

- I don't hear much from the customer.

- I know we have to work much smarter.

- I have some ideas for redesigning the work.

- I know what they want and am committed to it.

Check the actions that interest you:

■ If you do not know who your customers are, find out. Even if you are part of a larger team or group, know who consumes the products or services you perform.

■ Sketch the value chain of your services—how the work you perform flows—from internal customer to the ultimate customer: the external purchaser/user.

■ Ask the next person in the value chain, "How am I serving your needs?" or "How can I give you more of what you need?" And listen.

■ Pay attention to service quality scores no matter what your position. Find out how you can make these measures more meaningful to you, and improve them.

■ Meet with your customers personally. Ask broad questions, not just about how they like the service: "If you could have anything you wanted from this service, what would it be?" Do not try to convince customers you have the right thing. Listen and let them convince you.

■ Examine your current assumptions and beliefs about how to bring increased value to the customer. Explore options that go beyond the processes and procedures that have been in place up till now.

■ When you can, include some customers in your meetings to tell you what they want and what they like.

■ In job interviews show interest in who the customer is and how the customer is served. Letting a potential employer know that you are focused on the customer will give you points in a selection decision.

4 | HIGH PERFORMANCE

Reach for high performance standards:

How well are you performing on a day-to-day basis in the opinion of your customer and your supervisor?

■ I don't know truthfully.

■ I have a general idea.

■ I get good feedback.

■ I am continuously improving performance.

How clear are you about redesigning your current job to deliver more value to the customer and the company?

- I am not clear at all.
- I know people are talking about it.
- I can see where improvements and savings can be made.
- I am doing everything I can to make the job better.

Check the actions that interest you:

- In any unit in which you work, stay on top of the customer-driven goals at all times. If unclear, do whatever you can to get them clarified. Know how these goals will be measured.

- Keep track of your accomplishments, activities, wins, losses. Get regular 360-degree feedback about whether and how your performance is measuring up. Remember, the fact that a supervisor is not saying anything is not evidence of satisfaction with or approval of your work.

- Keep looking at how a job is structured. Is there an easier way to do the work? Is every step needed? Can more be delivered with less? Don't be afraid to make suggestions.

- Organize your time so that you know how to be most efficient. Keep meetings down to the essential action items that will produce results. Avoid distractions and interruptions.

- Be introspective about how you are doing your job. If you see areas for personal improvement, don't wait for someone else to bring it up. Find a good coach or mentor to give you advice.

5 | SELF-DIRECTION

Take action to have what you want in your future:

How frequently do you take initiative in learning about new parts of the company that are expanding?

- I don't care anymore.
- I wait to be told.
- I ask good questions occasionally.
- I am regularly seeking new information.

Are you making contacts within and outside the company (if still employed) to build an active network for possible future job relocation?

- ▦ I mostly know people I work with.

- ▦ I have been contacting others in the company.

- ▦ I have found people who can introduce me to others.

- ▦ I stay in touch with a number of people outside the company who can help me relocate if I were to leave my current company.

Check the actions that interest you:

- ▦ Stay alert to the directions of various industries that interest you by speaking to others who could know, by reading industry publications, by watching trends in related industries, and by using your imagination. Use logic and information to find likely directions that will be driven by customer and shareholder needs.

- ▦ Set personal job targets for the future. Study those job targets to find out what skills are required and who could be hiring for these positions.

- ▦ Keep your regular resume prepared for responding to opportunities inside and outside your company (if still employed).

- ▦ Build a list of contacts inside and outside the firm. Contact them informally to keep abreast of potential employment opportunities.

- ▦ Call people within your current company (if still employed) to seek out as much direct information on future job opportunities as possible.

- ▦ Read job postings, internal memos, and E-mail to see what jobs are becoming available within the company. Respond aggressively.

- ▦ Review the Writing Letters section on pages 56–59 and be ready to send out resumes with a personalized cover letter that will increase readability.

- ▦ Use your own writings from this book to practice giving positive descriptions of yourself.

- ▦ Keep notes of your assignments and achievements so they can be easily organized into a resume: internal and/or external.

- ▦ Visit your local library and ask for recommendations on career development and job change materials.

WORKSHEETS

Describing Capability

Your capabilities and skills are at the center of your employability. The more different things you can do well, the more employable you are. You can be flexible in assignments taking advantage of a wide range of opportunity. There are three categories for describing capability: skills for earning, qualities for leadership, and goals for learning. All three build your employability and keep you moving along with changing market needs.

Take plenty of time to evaluate your developed and developing talents. Stretch a little and identify the skills you *have* and those you will *need to develop* for the future.

CATEGORY I

SKILLS FOR EARNING

Think about future jobs or work assignments you would like. What skills are required for earning a good living and achieving success? Check the skills that apply below.

- doing physical or manual work (fix, assemble, build . . .)
- persuading or managing people (sell, manage, influence . . .)
- helping or counseling people (counsel, listen, care . . .)
- using artistic skills (draw, compose, act . . .)
- working with numbers (calculate, process, work with finances . . .)
- using language (write, present, teach . . .)
- using logical thinking (plan, research, organize . . .)
- using intuitive thinking (create, design . . .)
- being observant or visual (classify, diagnose . . .)

Now identify the specific skills you are capable of even if you have not yet had experience. Suggestions are provided.

Being successful in my future requires that I be able to:

1. _____
2. _____
3. _____
4. _____
5. _____
6. _____
7. _____
8. _____
9. _____
10. _____
11. _____
12. _____
13. _____
14. _____
15. _____
16. _____
17. _____
18. _____
19. _____
20. _____

SUGGESTIONS

- make face-to-face sales presentations
- conduct employee performance evaluations
- supervise people
- plan sales strategies
- use available personnel and materials resources effectively
- negotiate specifications and prices with suppliers
- manage people effectively
- negotiate with company and/or union officials
- prepare and manage scheduling
- teach individuals and work groups
- counsel personal problems
- show sensitivity/empathy
- teach and support
- train/instruct
- install electrical equipment and products
- install nonelectrical equipment
- service electrical and/or electronic equipment
- service mechanical equipment
- repair equipment
- test and ensure electrical and electronic equipment
- install cable
- operate machinery
- build and maintain facilities
- manually move, rearrange, and deliver material and equipment
- design advertising and promotional material
- design graphics and artwork
- develop audio and visual materials
- generate savings ideas
- develop financial plans, objectives, budgets, forecasts

- manage expenses/budget
- manage financial resources
- perform audits
- process bills
- decide product pricing
- solve accounting and payroll problems
- manage equipment inventory
- complete market analysis
- prepare written reports
- translate foreign languages
- deliver oral performance feedback
- deliver speeches
- communicate with/between speech- or hearing-impaired people
- deliver training/seminars externally to customers or others
- write operations manuals
- write and prepare proposals and presentations
- write newspaper, magazine, journal articles, news releases
- write contracts, bids, requests for proposal
- conduct staff meetings
- facilitate regional teams
- translate customer requests into service orders
- make presentations
- analyze customer business information
- analyze market research data, marketing information
- analyze competitor and competitive information
- analyze sales/marketing opportunities, leads, and potential
- analyze advertising and promotion plans
- analyze product and service performance data
- analyze employee performance
- file documents

- research customers' needs
- select outside contractors
- plan public relations activities
- write a business plan
- develop new-product markets
- organize labor, legal, and regulatory matters
- organize meetings, seminars, workshops, and training
- organize/coordinate data, information, and reports
- research and review documents, databases, and information
- conduct interviews
- interpret laws
- provide technical support

CATEGORY 2

QUALITIES FOR LEADERSHIP

In addition to specific skills, your employability is enhanced when demonstrating your qualities as a self-starter and leader. We've organized these qualities into four areas.

Spirit: Taking responsibility to maximize one's own interest in and enthusiasm for a particular strategic function or business. Increasing the morale of others as well.

Vision: Thinking in broad and innovative ways. Creating a compelling vision. Promoting continuous learning.

Relationship: Engaging with others to promote extraordinary relationships with customers, suppliers, and one another.

Performance: Providing superior service to customers while leading business operations. Always keeping to high personal standards.

Consider your ability to add value to situations that are beneficial to an organization and to its customers. In what ways are you accountable to generate results? List your top leadership qualities.

Being successful as a leader requires that I be able to:

1. _____
2. _____
3. _____
4. _____
5. _____
6. _____
7. _____
8. _____
9. _____
10. _____
11. _____
12. _____
13. _____
14. _____
15. _____
16. _____
17. _____
18. _____
19. _____
20. _____

SUGGESTIONS

- build strong relationships with employees, customers, and suppliers
- resolve conflicts
- coordinate plans and communicate effectively

- enhance the quality standards of suppliers
- build coalitions, inside and outside the company
- openly recognize others' contributions without promoting heroics
- provide and oversee developmental opportunities for others
- inspire strong feelings of commitment and dedication in others
- show genuine sensitivity to and interest in others
- take responsibility when appropriate
- give rewards and make decisions in an overt manner
- give rewards and make decisions based on articulated criteria
- consistently seek "win-win" situations
- frequently give candid and constructive feedback to employees
- motivate people to recognize their highest potential
- expect the best in others
- guide others to excel despite changes due to reorganization
- state novel ideas in a compelling manner
- clarify corporate strategies and their importance to the job at hand
- use metaphors and analogies to illustrate abstract points
- provide clear explanations of complex or technical issues
- communicate with conviction
- persuasively articulate new paradigms that help employees
- consistently "see the big picture"
- articulate how visions can be reached
- help others excel despite an environment of paradoxes
- generate imaginative, novel solutions to corporate problems
- question the usefulness of habits and traditions
- encourage discussion of new ideas
- challenge assumptions
- teach others
- follow others when they initiate change to solve a business need
- focus on possibilities rather than problems

- interact effectively with a variety of people and situations
- continually advance my understanding of pluralism
- be a role model for all behavior related to pluralism
- relentlessly apply the values of pluralism to work challenges
- aggressively pursue new learning experiences for self and others
- question beliefs and promote experimentation
- welcome challenges from others
- seek feedback and ideas from others
- understand business challenges from a universal point of view
- balance short- and long-term perspectives
- be multilingual or otherwise knowledgeable about other cultures
- have international work experience
- take initiative to contribute to the community
- recognize community involvement as a developmental opportunity
- exude authenticity
- inspire trust
- consistently model honest and ethical behavior
- behave consistently across words and actions
- reward honesty in others
- fully utilize the skills of others
- create situations where my own skills are fully utilized
- identify exceptional talents or knowledge bases of others
- allocate work to tap those special skills
- nurture the self-esteem of others and myself
- communicate very high expectations for myself and others
- foster the expression of enthusiasm, energy, and creativity
- promote an "abundance mentality"
- take myself lightly and ease tension through humor
- manage stress level so that it doesn't interfere with my job
- form amusing insights

GOALS FOR LEARNING

The Goals for Learning are designed to help you look ahead to future work and identify what you need to learn or improve upon so that you can be better prepared to successfully achieve your ideals.

Return to your skills and qualities lists and select up to five items that you can target for immediate development. Complete a Learning Goal for each. Make these goals as specific as possible and only list those you are willing to undertake.

LEARNING GOAL 1

Skill/quality to further learn/develop:_____

_____

A year from now, how do you want to see your abilities in this skill/quality?

_____

_____

What actions can you take to start?

▩ find someone who can help   ▩ read books or other materials

▩ apply for a scholarship   ▩ practice on my own

▩ take a training program   ▩ other

List specific actions and targeted completion dates:

ACTIONS TO TAKE   BY WHEN

_____   _____

_____   _____

_____   _____

_____   _____

LEARNING GOAL 2

Skill/quality to further learn/develop:_____

_____

A year from now, how do you want to see your abilities in this skill/
quality?

_____

_____

What actions can you take to start?

- find someone who can help   - read books or other materials
- apply for a scholarship   - practice on my own
- take a training program   - other

List specific actions and targeted completion dates:

ACTIONS TO TAKE   BY WHEN

_____   _____

_____   _____

_____   _____

_____   _____

LEARNING GOAL 3

Skill/quality to further learn/develop:_____

_____

A year from now, how do you want to see your abilities in this skill/
quality?

_____

_____

What actions can you take to start?

- [ ] find someone who can help
- [ ] apply for a scholarship
- [ ] take a training program
- [ ] read books or other materials
- [ ] practice on my own
- [ ] other

List specific actions and targeted completion dates:

ACTIONS TO TAKE	BY WHEN
_____	_____
_____	_____
_____	_____
_____	_____

LEARNING GOAL 4

Skill/quality to further learn/develop:_____

_____

A year from now, how do you want to see your abilities in this skill/ quality?

_____

_____

What actions can you take to start?

- [ ] find someone who can help
- [ ] apply for a scholarship
- [ ] take a training program
- [ ] read books or other materials
- [ ] practice on my own
- [ ] other

List specific actions and targeted completion dates:

ACTIONS TO TAKE   BY WHEN

_____   _____

_____   _____

_____   _____

_____   _____

LEARNING GOAL 5

Skill/quality to further learn/develop:_____

_____

A year from now, how do you want to see your abilities in this skill/quality?

_____

_____

What actions can you take to start?

- find someone who can help
- read books or other materials
- apply for a scholarship
- practice on my own
- take a training program
- other

List specific actions and targeted completion dates:

ACTIONS TO TAKE   BY WHEN

_____   _____

_____   _____

_____   _____

_____   _____

WORKSHEETS

Describing Results

A result is an accomplishment you have produced or delivered. To a potential employer, results back up and prove your skills and qualities, competencies and capabilities.

People mistakenly list duties or activities on their resume: "Responsible for dispatching technicians to respond to service calls." A result is what happened as a consequence of that duty or activity: "Improved customer satisfaction by reducing the time to respond to their needs."

Answer the following questions about results you produced in your current or most recent and your past jobs. The statements you write can be used in your resume. Suggestion: Photocopy these worksheets for as many drafts as you may need, and use pencil.

CURRENT OR MOST RECENT POSITION

_____–present (or end date) _____ (position title)

(employer/location)

_____

What is something you have done on this job of which you are proud?

I have _____

_____

What is something you have done on this job that thoroughly satisfied a customer (external or internal)?

I have _____

_____

_____

What is something you have done on this job that helped increase the quality of the product or service the company delivers?

I have _____

_____

What is something you have done on this job that was valuable for others?

I have _____

_____

What is something you did on this job that improved the way work was being done?

I have _____

_____

What else did you accomplish on this job?

I have _____

_____

PREVIOUS POSITION

_____-_____   _____ (position title)

_____ (employer/location)

What is something you have done on this job of which you are proud?

I have _____

_____

What is something you have done on this job that thoroughly satisfied a customer (external or internal)?

I have _____

_____

What is something you have done on this job that helped increase the quality of the product or service the company delivers?

I have _____

_____

What is something you have done on this job that was valuable for others?

I have _____

_____

What is something you did on this job that improved the way work was being done?

I have _____

_____

What else did you accomplish on this job?

I have _____

_____

PREVIOUS POSITION

_____-_____ _____ (position title)

_____ (employer/location)

What is something you have done on this job of which you are proud?

I have _____

_____

What is something you have done on this job that thoroughly satisfied a customer (external or internal)?

I have _____

_____

What is something you have done on this job that helped increase the quality of the product or service the company delivers?

I have _____

_____

What is something you have done on this job that was valuable for others?

I have _____

_____

What is something you did on this job that improved the way work was being done?

I have _____

_____

What else did you accomplish on this job?

I have _____

_____

Other Results

List any other result you produced in past jobs, volunteer work, or other activities. Pay particular attention to examples when you may have:

- met customer expectations
- improved work processes
- reduced costs
- increased revenues
- increased quality
- built an organization's capability

I have _____

_____

I have _____

_____

I have _____

_____

I have _____

_____

I have _____

_____

SAMPLE RESUME PARAGRAPHS

On the following pages we have included sample paragraphs relating to occupational titles not necessarily covered in all of the catalog resumes. Use them for reference in creating your own resume.

Account Executive ▪ Plan, coordinate, and direct advertising campaign for diverse client base of advertising agency. Consult with clients to determine advertising requirements and budgetary limitations, utilizing knowledge of product or service to be advertised, media capabilities, and audience characteristics.

Consult with creative staff, photographers, and other media production specialists to select media to be used and to estimate costs. Submit proposal, including estimated budget for client approval.

Coordinate marketing research, copywriting, layout, media-buying, display, and promotional activities to successfully implement changes.

Activities Planner—College ▪ Provide motivation and successful sales targeting for a team of assistant box office managers. Manage ticket sales coordinating mini box office to open in time segments so that tickets are available sixteen hours per day in various locations. Create on-line database to track ticket sales and seating availability. Schedule sports events during academic years. Produce large sellout for dances and other social events.

Administrative Assistant ▪ Provide support to management by handling all routine and administrative work such as coordinating office services, preparing budgets and cash flow statements, maintaining records, tracing information, coordinating details of business trips, and organizing special projects. Communicate with counterparts in other departments and retrieve information through establishing a network. Conduct research, provide facts and statistics for reports. Read and condense lengthy documents.

Art Director ▪ Formulate concepts and supervise staff in executing layout designs for artwork and copy to be presented by visual communications media, such as magazines, books, newspapers, television, on-line services, posters, and packaging. Review illustrative material and consult with client or individual responsible for presentation regarding budget, background information, objectives, presentation approaches, style, techniques, and related production factors.

Formulate layout and design concept, select and secure suitable illustrative material, or conceive and delegate production of material and detail to artists and photographers. Assign and direct staff members to develop design concepts into art layouts and prepare layouts for printing. Review, approve, and present final layouts to client or department head for approval.

Biotechnologist ▪ Conduct research and development activities to augment knowledge of living organisms. Employ genetic knowledge and technology to recombine the genetic material of plants and animals. Perform studies and assay development for new drug discovery projects. Conduct computer-assisted analyses of data. Monitor and report on progress of ongoing clinical studies. Utilize computer networking and videoconferencing to do research with individuals in other locations.

Certified Public Accountant ▪ Examine clients' financial records and reports and attest to their conformity with standards of preparation and reporting. Prepare income tax returns and advise clients of the tax advantages and disadvantages of certain business decisions. Consult on a variety of matters, such as revising the clients' accounting systems to better meet their needs and advising clients on managing cash resources more profitably. Prepare financial reports to meet public disclosure requirements of stock exchanges, the SEC, and other regulatory bodies. Conduct internal audits of all financial reporting systems. Determine the feasibility of projects by developing internal rate of return analyses on the profitability of new working capital investments.

Computer Animator ▪ Create sophisticated computer graphics using supercomputers such as the Cray X-MP digital image producer. "Paint" on computer VDT via a digitizing tablet to enhance and speed the development of animation and other presentations. Draw electronically using a mouse cursor control. Store and retrieve two-dimensional images, text and lettering to be captured on slides, film, video, or hard copy. Create full and partial movement images incorporating digital images and sound clips.

Corporate Foundation Manager ▪ Administer the distribution of funding to nonprofit organizations. Meet with organizations seeking grants, administer requests, prepare agenda for corporate meeting, and follow up on gifts. Coordinate employee participations. Maintain approach consisting of a belief in cultural diversity in developing fund-raising projects. Act as a liaison with the community. Able to work in a fast-paced, dynamic environment, characterized by time restraints and budgeting requirements.

Maintain accounting records using computer spreadsheet software package.

Counseling Director ▪ Direct people engaged in providing educational and vocational guidance for students and graduates. Assign and evaluate work of personnel. Conduct in-service training program for professional staff. Coordinate counseling bureau with school and community services. Analyze counseling services and guidance procedures and techniques to improve quality of service. Develop database of employee profiles to track necessary counseling and training in order to create a means to track progress with individuals and the organization as a whole.

Counsel individuals and groups relative to personal and social problems, and educational and vocational objectives. Address community groups and faculty members to interpret counseling services. Supervise maintenance of occupational library for use by counseling personnel. Direct activities of testing and occupational service center. Supervise counseling staff and develop quarterly curriculum of pertinent issues to be addressed.

Dental Hygienist ▪ Provide preventive dental care and encourage patients to develop good oral hygiene skills. Evaluate patients' dental health. Remove calculus, stain, and plaque and apply caries-preventive agents such as fluoride and pit and fissure sealants. Instruct patients on plaque control. Expose and develop X rays. Place temporary fillings and periodontal dressings. Remove sutures. Polish and recontour amalgam restorations. Administer local anesthetics.

Drafter ▪ Prepare clear, complete, and accurate working plans and detailed drawings from rough or detailed sketches or notes for engineering or manufacturing purposes, according to specified dimensions. Make final drawing and specifications, checking dimension of parts, materials to be used, relation of one part to another, and relations of various parts to whole structure or project. Exercise manual skill in manipulation of triangle, T square, and other drafting tools or make drawings on video screens using **AUTOCAD RIZ** and Softdesk. Draw charts for representation of statistical data. Draw finished designs from sketches. Present drafts and schematics to clients. Interface with engineers and construction managers to ensure project feasibility. Utilize knowledge of various machines, engineering practices, mathematics, building materials, and other physical sciences to complete drawings.

Economist ▪ Utilize knowledge of economic relationships to advise businesses, government agencies, and others. Devise methods and procedures to obtain needed data, including sampling techniques, to conduct surveys. Employ econometric modeling to develop projections. Review and analyze data; prepare tables and charts; prepare clear, concise reports. Analyze the effect of tax law changes. Prepare economic and business forecasts. Provide information to support management decision-making process. Use on-line services to adjust and update forecasts and projections.

Editorial Assistant ▪ Prepare written material for publication. Review copy to detect errors in spelling, punctuation, and syntax. Verify facts, dates, and statistics, using standard reference sources. Assure that manuscripts conform to publisher's style and editorial policy and mark copy for typesetter, using standard symbols to indicate how type should be set.

Read galley and page proofs to detect errors and indicate corrections, using standard proofreading symbols. Confer with authors regarding changes made to manuscript. Select and crop photographs and illustrative materials to conform to space and subject matter requirements.

Educational Therapist ▪ Teach elementary and secondary school subjects to educationally challenged students with neurological or emotional disabilities in schools, institutions, or other specialized facilities. Plan curriculum and prepare lessons and other instructional materials to meet individual needs of students, considering such factors as physical, emotional, and educational levels of development. Instruct students in specific subject areas, such as English, mathematics, and geography.

Observe students for signs of disruptive behavior, such as violence, outbursts of temper, and episodes of destructiveness. Counsel students with regard to disruptive behavior, utilizing a variety of therapeutic methods. Confer with other staff members to plan programs designed to promote educational, physical, and social development of students.

Environmental Health Inspector ▪ Ensure that food, water, and air meet government standards. Check the cleanliness and safety of food and beverages produced in dairies and processing plants, served in restaurants, hospitals, and other institutions. Examine the handling, processing, and serving of food for compliance with sanitation rules and regulations.

Oversee the treatment and disposal of sewage and refuse. Examine places where there is danger of pollution. Collect samples of air and water for analysis. Determine the nature and cause of pollution and initiate action to stop it. Analyze environmental impact of new projects and its effect on project feasibility.

Fashion Coordinator ▪ Promote new fashions and coordinate promotional activities, such as fashion shows, to induce consumer acceptance. Study fashion and trade journals, travel to garment centers, attend fashion shows, and visit manufacturers and merchandise markets to obtain information on fashion trends. Consult with buying personnel to gain advice regarding types of fashions store will purchase and feature for season. Advise publicity and display departments of merchandise to be publicized.

Select garments and accessories to be shown at fashion shows. Provide information on current fashions, style trends, and use of accessories.

Contract with models, musicians, caterers, and others to manage staging of shows.

Guidance Director ▪ Organize, administer, and coordinate guidance program in public school system. Formulate guidance policies and procedures. Plan and conduct in-service training program for guidance workers and selected teachers. Plan and supervise testing program in school system and devise and direct use of records, reports, and other material essential to program.

Supervise school placement service. Establish and supervise maintenance of occupational libraries in schools. Coordinate guidance activities with community agencies and other areas of school system. Conduct or supervise research studies to evaluate effectiveness of guidance program.

Guidance Navigation Control Engineer ▪ Develop basic design concepts used in the design, development, and validation of electromechanical GNC systems for stabilizing, navigating, and maneuvering vehicles in flight. Provide analysis for satellites and space launch vehicles. Employ knowledge and experience in rigid-body dynamics, guidance, digital flight controls, and flight control computer software validation. Use supercomputers to analyze and create computer-generated feasibility studies of new designs.

Industrial Electronic Equipment Repair ▪ Install and repair electronic equipment used in industrial automated equipment controls, missile control systems, medical and diagnostic equipment, transmitters and antennas. Set up and service an industrial robotics system. Use testing equipment to ensure everything is functioning properly before the customer takes charge of the equipment. Perform preventative maintenance; check, clean, and repair equipment periodically. Create a computer database of all equipment indicating the date and its condition, and when it is to be serviced again. Determine the cause of equipment breakdown using tools such as voltmeter, ohmmeter, signal generator, ammeter, and oscilloscope. Repair and replace defective components and wiring, and calibrate the equipment.

Internal Auditor ▪ Examine and evaluate the firm's financial and information systems, management procedures, and internal controls. Ensure that records are accurate and controls adequate to protect against fraud and waste. Review the company's operations and evaluate their efficiency, effectiveness, and compliance with corporate policies, laws, and government regulations. Conduct audits to determine an accountability of assets and any areas where improvements can be made. Monitor controls in computer software to ensure reliability of systems and integrity of data. Correct problems with software systems and develop special programs to meet unique needs.

Lobbyist ▪ Contact and confer with members of legislature and other holders of public office to persuade them to support legislation favorable to clients' interests. Study proposed legislation to determine possible effect on interest of clients, who may be a person, specific group, or general public. Confer with legislators and officials to emphasize supposed weaknesses or merits of specific bills to influence passage, defeat, or amendment of measure or introduction of legislation more favorable to clients' interests.

Contact individuals and groups having similar interests in order to encourage them also to contact legislators and present views. Prepare news releases and informational pamphlets and conduct news conferences in order to state clients' views and to inform public of features of proposed legislation considered desirable or undesirable.

Management Consultant ▪ Help solve a vast array of organizational problems. Consult with client to define the nature and extent of the project. Collect and review data. Work with senior management to receive feedback and determine needs assessments. Analyze statistics and other data, interview employees, observe the operations on a day-to-day basis. Utilize knowledge of theory, principles, or technology of specific discipline or field of specialization to determine solutions. Prepare recommendations and write a report of findings. Create a basis of determining real, measurable means of judging impact of any recommended changes. Make formal oral presentations to the client. Assist in the implementation of proposals.

Management Trainee ▪ Perform assigned duties, under close direction of experienced personnel, to gain knowledge and experience required for promotion to management positions. Receive training and perform duties in departments, such as credit, customer relations, accounting, or sales to become familiar with line and staff functions that affect each phase of business. Observe and study techniques and traits of experienced workers in order to acquire knowledge of methods, procedures, and standards required for performance of departmental duties.

Manager, Retail Store ▪ Manage retail store engaged in selling specific line of merchandise, such as groceries, meat, liquor, apparel, jewelry, or furniture; related lines of merchandise, such as radios, televisions, and household appliances; or general line of merchandise.

Perform following duties personally or supervise staff performing duties. Plan and prepare work schedules and assign schedules and employees to specific duties. Formulate pricing policies on merchandise according to requirements for profitability of store operations. Coordinate sales promotion activities and prepare, or direct workers preparing, merchandise displays and advertising copy.

Supervise employees engaged in, or performing, sales work, taking of inventories, reconciling cash with sales receipts, keeping operating records, or preparing daily record of transactions for accountant. Create a database of all employees to monitor skill developments and set up development plans to ensure that they are meeting necessary organizational requirements for advancement. Order merchandise or prepare requisitions to replenish merchandise on hand. Ensure compliance of employees with established security, sales, and record-keeping procedures and practices.

Marketing Manager　Analyze and evaluate marketing research data and apply to customer base. Plan and develop marketing strategies. Coordinate with product management on product design. Develop and manage cross-product marketing materials. Design promotional programs; supervise training. Develop and manage budgets. Work with ad agencies, type houses, editors, printers, art directors, producers, and audiovisual studios. Coordinate public relations materials and execute press releases for new products. Oversee scheduling and participation in trade shows and seminars; develop required promotional materials. Develop tactical sales support materials. Participate in the development of business strategies. Responsible for quality and consistency of information and upkeep and distribution of marketing database information.

Mechanical Engineer　Design and develop power-producing machines such as internal combustion engines, steam and gas turbines and jet and rocket engines, refrigeration and air-conditioning equipment, robots, machine tools, materials-handling systems, and industrial production equipment. Direct and coordinate operation and repair activities. Use CAD and CAM programs to quickly develop products and scenarios for analyzing.

Medical Record Administrator　Plan, develop, and administer medical record systems for hospital, clinic, health center, or similar facility, to meet standards of accrediting and regulatory agencies. Collect and analyze patient and institutional data. Assist medical staff in evaluating quality of patient care and in developing criteria and methods for such evaluation.

Develop and implement policies and procedures for documenting, storing, and retrieving information and for processing medical-legal documents, insurance, and corresponding requests, in conformance with federal, state, and local statutes. Develop in-service educational materials and conduct instructional programs for health care personnel. Supervise staff in preparing and analyzing medical documents. Provide consultant services to health care facilities, health data systems, related health organizations, and governmental agencies. Engage in basic and applied research in health care field. Testify in court about records and record procedures. Train and supervise medical records staff.

Merchandise Manager　Formulate merchandising policies and coordinate merchandising activities in wholesale or retail establishment. Determine markup and markdown percentages necessary to ensure profit based on estimated budget, profit goals, and average rate of stock turnover. Determine amount of merchandise to be stocked and direct buyers in purchase of supplies for resale. Consult with other personnel to plan sales promotion programs. Create and maintain accurate inventory database system in order to reduce stockouts or overstocks.

Nuclear Medicine Technologist

Perform activities involving the use of radionuclides in the diagnosis and treatment of disease. Develop and administer procedures for the purchase, use, and disposal of radioactive nuclides. Calculate, prepare, and administer the correct dosage of radiopharmaceuticals for the patient to take. Operate the gamma scintillation scanner and other diagnostic imaging equipment and view the images on computer screen or film. Process cardiac function studies with the aid of a computer. Perform ultrasound scans, fluoroscopy, and X rays. Collect body specimens such as blood and urine and measure for radioactivity. Ensure that safety procedures required by the Nuclear Regulatory Commission are carefully followed. Do research and conduct laboratory studies. Maintain complete and accurate records using database and spreadsheet software.

Numerical Control Tool Programmer

Apply a broad knowledge of machinery operations, and the working properties of metal and plastic used to make parts. Analyze blueprints. Plan and design the sequence of machine operations and select proper cutting tools. Write the program in the language of the machine's controller using a CAD/CAM system.

Package Designer

Design containers for products, such as food, beverages, toiletries, cigarettes, and medicines. Confer with representatives of engineering, marketing, management, and other departments to determine packaging requirements and type of product market. Sketch design of container for specific product, considering factors such as attractiveness, convenience in handling and storing, distinctiveness for identification by consumer, and simplicity to minimize production costs.

Render design, including exterior markings and labels, using paints and brushes. Use graphic design programs to create initial package designs for presentations and templates for model designs. Typically fabricate model in paper, wood, glass, plastic, or metal, depending on material to be used in package. Make modifications required by approving authority.

Plant Engineer

Direct and coordinate, through engineering and supervisory personnel, activities concerned with design, construction, and maintenance of equipment in accordance with engineering principles and safety regulations. Maintain compliance with all OSHA requirements. Directly oversee maintenance of plant buildings. Coordinate resurveys, new designs, and maintenance schedules with operating requirements. Update database of all physical plant requirements, repair schedules, and future maintenance needs. Prepare bid sheets and contracts for construction and facilities acquisition. Test newly installed machines and equipment to ensure fulfillment of contract specifications.

Project Director ▪ Plan, direct, and coordinate activities of designated project to ensure that aims, goals, or objectives specified for project are accomplished in accordance with prescribed priorities, time limitations, and funding conditions. Use project coordinating software to ensure all timetables and schedules are met. Review project proposal plan and determine methods and procedures for its accomplishment. Develop staffing plan and establish work plan and schedules for each phase of project in accordance with time limitations and funding with project management software.

Recruit or request assignment of personnel. Confer with staff, designate responsibilities, and establish scope of authority. Direct and coordinate activities of project through delegated subordinates and establish budget control system. Review project reports on status of each phase and modify schedules as required. Prepare project status reports for management. Confer with project personnel to provide technical advice and to assist in solving problems.

Public Relations Representative ▪ Plan and conduct public relations program designed to create and maintain favorable public image for employer or client. Plan and direct development and communication of information designed to keep public informed of employer's programs, accomplishments, or point of view. Arrange for public relations effort in order to meet needs, objectives, and policies of individual, special interest group, business concern, nonprofit organization, or government agency, serving as in-house staff member or as outside consultant.

Prepare and distribute fact sheets, news releases, electronic mail, photographs, scripts, motion pictures, or tape recordings to media representatives and other persons who may be interested in learning about or publicizing employer's activities or message. Purchase advertising space and time as required. Set up special interest Web sites on the Internet. Arrange for and conduct public-contact programs designed to meet employer's objectives, utilizing knowledge of changing attitudes and opinions of consumers, client's employees, or other interest groups.

Promote goodwill through such publicity efforts as speeches, exhibits, films, tours, and question/answer sessions. Represent employer during community projects and at public, social, and business gatherings.

Research Nutritionist ▪ Conduct nutritional research to expand knowledge in one or more phases of dietetics. Plan, organize, and conduct programs in nutrition, foods, and food-service systems, evaluating and utilizing appropriate methodology and tools to carry out program. Study and analyze recent scientific discoveries in nutrition for application in current research, for development of tools for future research, and for interpretation to the public, using on-line services to keep up-to-date on new scientific data and nutritional developments. Communicate findings through reports and publications.

Residence Counselor ▪ Provide individual and group guidance services relative to problems of scholastic, educational, and personal-social nature to dormitory students. Suggest remedial or corrective actions to assist students in making better adjustments and in intelligent planning of life goals. Plan and direct program to orient new students and assist in their integration into campus life. Initiate and conduct group conferences to plan and discuss programs and policies related to assignment of quarters, social and recreational activities, and dormitory living. Supervise dormitory activities. Investigate reports of misconduct and attempt to resolve or eliminate cause of conflict.

Robot Technician ▪ Assemble robotic prototypes. Work from engineer's CAD/CAM or AUTOCAD blueprints and create the first working model of the robot. Discover and troubleshoot system malfunctions. Evaluate retooling requirement for new products. Create cost analyses for adapting automation systems for new-product design. Test and calibrate electronic test equipment.

Sales Manager ▪ Direct the firm's sales program. Assign sales territories and goals. Establish training program for sales representatives. Oversee regional and local sales managers and staffs in larger firms utilizing sales-tracking software. Maintain on-line contact with dealers and distributors. Analyze sales statistics gathered by staff to monitor preferences and decide which products to continue or discontinue.

Order merchandise, supplies, and equipment as necessary. Ensure that merchandise is correctly priced and displayed. Prepare sales and inventory databases and reports. Approve checks for payment of merchandise and issue credit or cash refund on returned merchandise. Plan department layout on merchandise or advertising display.

Sociologist ▪ Study human society and social behavior by examining group and social institutions that people form. Study origin, growth, behavior, and interaction of groups. Collect information, assess validity, and analyze results. Conduct surveys or engage in direct observation to gather data. Utilize statistical and computer techniques in research. Evaluate social and welfare programs.

Student Affairs Director ▪ Plan and arrange social, cultural, and recreational activities of various student groups according to university policies and regulations. Meet with student and faculty groups to plan activities. Evaluate programs and suggest modifications. Utilize scheduling software to prevent overlapping and coordinate activities with sports and other university programs.

Contact caterers, entertainers, decorators, and others to arrange for scheduled events. Conduct orientation program for new students with other members of faculty and staff. Advise student groups on financial status of and methods for improving their organizations. Promote student participation in social, cultural, and recreational activities.

Systems Analyst ▪ Plan and develop methods for computerizing business and scientific tasks or improving the computer system already in use. Discuss data processing problems with managers, specialists, or end-user focus groups to determine exact nature of the problem. Design goals of the system and use techniques such as mathematical model building, sampling, and cost accounting to plan the system.

Develop the design and prepare charts and diagrams that describe it in terms management can understand. Prepare cost-benefit analysis and return on investment. Determine computer hardware and software requirements. Prepare specifications for programmers. Design forms required to collect and distribute information. Develop better procedures and adapt the system to handle additional types of data. Research and devise new methods for systems analysis.

Teacher's Aide ▪ Assist teaching staff of public or private elementary or secondary school by performing any combination of tasks in classroom. Help instruct children under the guidance and supervision of the teacher. Prepare lesson outline and plan where appropriate and submit it for review. Prepare and develop various teaching aids, such as bibliographies, charts, and graphs. Help and supervise students in classroom, cafeteria, and school yard. Record grades, set up equipment, help prepare materials for instruction. Grade tests and papers, check homework, and keep health and attendance records.

Telecommunications Specialist ▪ Provide expert advice to companies on putting together the most efficient, effective, and economical system. Be familiar with the telephone and data communications systems available from different manufacturers and the many ways to lease transmission lines. Have knowledge of computerized telephone systems, computerized mail, videoconferencing, teletext, telex, facsimile, scanners, and OCR software. Analyze the current system and the company's needs. Select and design a system to meet these needs as well as the ability to expand and upgrade the system as business needs demand. Supervise the system installation. Establish a framework for its economical operation.

Urban and Regional Planner ▪ Develop programs to provide for the future growth for revitalization of urban, suburban, and rural communities and their regions. Examine community facilities to ensure they will meet the demands placed on them. Keep abreast of economic and legal issues and changes in housing and building codes and environmental regulations. Design new transportation systems and parking facilities. Project long-range needs for housing, transport, business, and industrial sites that may develop as a result of population growth and economic and social changes.

Analyze and propose alternative ways to achieve more efficient and attractive urban areas. Prepare detailed studies that show the current use of land for residential, business, and community purposes. Provide information on the types of industries in the community, the characteristics of the population, the employment and economic trends. Propose ways to use undeveloped or underutilized land and design the layout of the recommended facilities and buildings. Demonstrate how the plan could be implemented and its costs.

Water and Wastewater Treatment Plant Officer Control the processes and equipment used to remove solid materials, chemicals, and microorganisms from water or to render them harmless. Read and interpret meters and gauges and adjust controls. Operate chemical feeding devices. Take samples of water and perform chemical and biological laboratory analyses. Test and adjust the chlorine levels in wastewater. Make minor repairs to valves, pumps, and other equipment. Use computers to help monitor equipment and processes. Read and interpret results.

WORKSHEETS

Writing Resumes

CHOOSING THE BEST FORMAT FOR EACH SITUATION

There are a variety of ways to organize your resume so that it elicits the response you seek from prospective employers.

- The **chronological resume** organizes your work experience chronologically.
- The **functional resume** describes functions or areas of skill, avoiding a strict reliance on chronological history.
- The **targeted resume** aims at a specific job or work opportunity and organizes information in terms of what is needed for the job rather than what you've done in the past.
- The **capabilities resume—internal** focuses on a well-researched actual or potential need within an organization for which you're already working. Its layout is similar to the targeted resume, but it includes its own built-in cover letter.

For each of the four formats, put a check next to any statements below that pertain to you.

CHRONOLOGICAL RESUME
(Emphasizes career growth and work experience.)

ADVANTAGES

▨ Staying in the same field as past jobs.

▨ Job history shows real growth and development.

▨ Past titles are highly impressive.

▨ Name of last employer is important.

▨ Want to emphasize employment history.

DISADVANTAGES

▨ Looking for your first job.

▨ Changing career goals or work focus.

▨ Have been absent from the job market for a while.

▨ Want to deemphasize dates.

▨ Changed employers too frequently.

FUNCTIONAL RESUME
(Emphasizes functions or areas of skill.)

ADVANTAGES

▨ Looking for your first job.

▨ Changing career goals or work focus.

▨ Skills are more impressive than work history.

▨ Have been absent from the job market for a while.

▨ Changed employers too frequently.

DISADVANTAGES

▨ Have performed a limited number of skills in past jobs.

▨ Want to emphasize employment history.

▨ Job history shows real growth and development.

▨ Name of last employer is important.

TARGETED RESUME
(Highlights capabilities/skills and supporting accomplishments for a specific job target.)

ADVANTAGES

▨ Want to make an impressive case for a specific job target.

▨ Very clear about job direction or skill focus.

▨ Willing to write a resume for each job target.

▨ Have skills, but not necessarily long, impressive history in those skills.

DISADVANTAGES

░ *Not* clear about job targets.

░ Only want one all-purpose resume.

░ *Not* certain of skills and capabilities.

░ Just starting, and have limited experience.

CAPABILITIES RESUME—INTERNAL

(Highlights capabilities/skills and supporting accomplishments for a specific internal assignment or position.)

ADVANTAGES

░ Want to make an impressive case for a specific job assignment.

░ Very clear about work direction or skills focus.

░ Willing to write a resume for each targeted assignment.

░ Have skills, as well as history to demonstrate those skills.

DISADVANTAGES

░ *Not* clear about new developing internal needs.

░ Only want one all-purpose resume—internal or external.

░ *Not* certain of skills and capabilities.

░ Newly hired, with limited experience.

Review the advantages and disadvantages of each format. Put two checks next to issues that are very important to you. Select the format that is best for you. If you are still unclear about which format to choose, try writing your resume using different formats and compare the results. Start with the format *easiest* for you to write.

DRAFTING THE RESUME

Use the following pages to write a draft resume. Find the pages for the resume format you selected and enter your personal information into the different resume sections. Use additional paper as needed. Photocopy these worksheets as needed.

CHRONOLOGICAL RESUME (DRAFT)

Name & Address _____

_____

Phone _____

Fax/E-mail _____

WORK EXPERIENCE

(Start with your most recent job and work back in time.)

Dates _____ Job Title _____

Employer _____ City/State _____
(Review the accomplishments you wrote for this position on the Describing Results worksheets. Select those that directly demonstrate your fitness for the job.)

Selected
Results _____

_____

_____

_____

_____

_____

Dates _____ Job Title _____

Employer _____ City/State _____
(Review the accomplishments you wrote for this position on the Describing Results worksheets. Select those that most directly demonstrate your fitness for the job.)

Selected
Results _____

_____

_____

_____

_____

_____

Dates _____ Job Title _____

Employer _____ City/State _____

(Review the accomplishments you wrote for this position on the Describing Results worksheets. Select those that directly demonstrate your fitness for the job.)

Select
Results
_____

_____

_____

_____

_____

_____

(Use additional pages as needed.)

EDUCATION

Dates _____ School _____ City/State ___

Degree _____ Major _____

Selected

Accomplishments _____

(optional) _____

Dates _____ School _____ City/State ___

Degree _____ Major _____

Selected

Accomplishments _____

(optional) _____

OTHER SUPPORTING INFORMATION

(Include any additional information that supports your fitness for the job: affiliations/associations, publications, volunteer experience, language proficiency, training programs, etc.)

_____

_____

_____

FUNCTIONAL RESUME (DRAFT)

Name & Address _____

_____

Phone _____

Fax/E-mail _____

FUNCTIONAL HEADING

(Describe below all supporting achievements, accomplishments, or results that you have produced in this functional area. From the Describing Results worksheets, select those that directly demonstrate your fitness for the job.)

_____

_____

_____

_____

_____

FUNCTIONAL HEADING

(Describe below all supporting achievements, accomplishments, or results that you have produced in this functional area. From the Describing Results worksheets, select those that directly demonstrate your fitness for the job.)

_____

_____

_____

_____

_____

FUNCTIONAL HEADING

(Describe below all supporting achievements, accomplishments, or results that you have produced in this functional area. From the Describing Results worksheets, select those that directly demonstrate your fitness for the job.)

_____

_____

_____

_____

_____

(Use additional functional headings as needed.)

WORK EXPERIENCE
(Start with your most recent job and work back in time.)

Dates _____ Job Title _____

Employer _____ City/State _____

Dates _____ Job Title _____

Employer _____ City/State _____

Dates _____ Job Title _____

Employer _____ City/State _____

EDUCATION

Dates _____ School _____ City/State ____

Degree _____ Major _____

Selected

Accomplishments _____

(optional) _____

Dates _____ School _____ City/State ____

Degree _____ Major _____

Selected

Accomplishments _____

(optional) _____

OTHER SUPPORTING INFORMATION
*(Include any additional information that supports your fitness for the job:
affiliations/associations, publications, volunteer experience, language proficiency,
training programs, etc.)*

_____

_____

TARGETED RESUME (DRAFT)

Name & Address _____

_____

Phone _____

Fax/E-mail _____

JOB TARGET

(A short description of a job title or work assignment; okay to include function or industry.)

_____

CAPABILITIES

(Review your inventory of top skills and qualities from the Describing Capability worksheets. Select those that you can do or could do in performing your targeted job.)

- _____
- _____
- _____
- _____
- _____

(Use additional bulleted lines as needed.)

ACCOMPLISHMENTS

(Review your accomplishments from the Describing Results worksheets. Select those that demonstrate what you have done to produce results in your targeted job area.)

- _____
- _____
- _____
- _____
- _____

(Use additional bulleted lines as needed.)

WORK EXPERIENCE

(Start with your most recent job and work back in time.)

Dates _____ Job Title _____

Employer _____ City/State _____

Dates _____ Job Title _____

Employer _____ City/State _____

Dates _____ Job Title _____

Employer _____ City/State _____

EDUCATION

Dates _____ School _____ City/State ____

Degree _____ Major _____

Selected
Accomplishments _____
(optional)

Dates _____ School _____ City/State ____

Degree _____ Major _____

Selected
Accomplishments _____
(optional)

OTHER SUPPORTING INFORMATION

(Include any additional information that supports your fitness for the job: affiliations/associations, publications, volunteer experience, language proficiency, training programs, etc.)

_____

_____

_____

_____

CAPABILITIES RESUME—INTERNAL (DRAFT)

DATE: _____

TO: Name _____ Title _____

          Department _____ Ext/E-mail _____

FROM: Name _____ Title _____

          Department _____ Ext/E-mail _____

INTRODUCTION

(A cover statement detailing an understanding of current issues, directions, functions; and your assertion of yourself as capable of joining another/others in solving problems, resolving issues, initiating or completing projects, etc.)

_____

_____

_____

_____

(Use additional lines as needed.)

CAPABILITIES

(List specific capabilities and core competencies that back up the introductory cover statement and that can also be specifically described in the Accomplishments section.)

Some of my capabilities/core competencies are:

- _____
- _____
- _____
- _____
- _____

(Use additional bulleted lines as needed.)

ACCOMPLISHMENTS
(List specific results, achievements, and accomplishments that demonstrate and back up the capabilities/competencies, as well as the introductory cover statement.)

A partial list of my demonstrated results:

- _____
- _____
- _____
- _____
- _____

(Use additional bulleted lines as needed.)

RECENT HISTORY
(Fill in the blank with name of current employer. Best to go no farther back than five to seven years.)

Title _____ Dates _____

Department/Division _____

Title _____ Dates _____

Department/Division _____

(Use additional lines as needed.)

RECENT TRAINING/DEVELOPMENT

Course (internal or external) _____ Dates _____

Certification/Skill Level _____

(Use additional lines as needed.)

At the bottom of the resume, note that you have attached a standard chronological or functional resume:

Previous work history, education/training: see attached resume.

If you are not attaching a standard resume, add additional supporting information, if needed, on a second page:

OTHER SUPPORTING INFORMATION

(Include any additional information that supports your fitness for the job or assignment: affiliations/associations, publications, volunteer experience, language proficiency, etc.)

_____

_____

_____

_____

_____

WORKSHEETS

Listing Your Contacts and Using Your Networks

YOUR PERSONAL NETWORK

Includes family, relatives, friends, neighbors, clergy. Can provide moral support, personal feedback, financial assistance, etc.

Name _____

Position _____

Organization _____

Address _____

City, State, ZIP _____

Phone/Fax/E-mail _____

Notes _____

Name _____

Position _____

Organization _____

Address _____

City, State, ZIP _____

Phone/Fax/E-mail _____

Notes _____

YOUR PERSONAL NETWORK (continued)

Name _____

Position _____

Organization _____

Address _____

City, State, ZIP _____

Phone/Fax/E-mail _____

Notes _____

Name _____

Position _____

Organization _____

Address _____

City, State, ZIP _____

Phone/Fax/E-mail _____

Notes _____

Name _____

Position _____

Organization _____

Address _____

City, State, ZIP _____

Phone/Fax/E-mail _____

Notes _____

Name _____

Position _____

Organization _____

Address _____

City, State, ZIP _____

Phone/Fax/E-mail _____

Notes _____

YOUR PERSONAL NETWORK (continued)

Name _____

Position _____

Organization _____

Address _____

City, State, ZIP _____

Phone/Fax/E-mail _____

Notes _____

Name _____

Position _____

Organization _____

Address _____

City, State, ZIP _____

Phone/Fax/E-mail _____

Notes _____

YOUR PROFESSIONAL NETWORK

Includes current or former coworkers and supervisors, teachers/professors, authors, consultants. Can provide contacts in your field, introductions and referrals, information on trends, career advice.

Name _____

Position _____

Organization _____

Address _____

City, State, ZIP _____

Phone/Fax/E-mail _____

Notes _____

YOUR PROFESSIONAL NETWORK (continued)

Name _____

Position _____

Organization _____

Address _____

City, State, ZIP _____

Phone/Fax/E-mail _____

Notes _____

Name _____

Position _____

Organization _____

Address _____

City, State, ZIP _____

Phone/Fax/E-mail _____

Notes _____

Name _____

Position _____

Organization _____

Address _____

City, State, ZIP _____

Phone/Fax/E-mail _____

Notes _____

Name _____

Position _____

Organization _____

Address _____

City, State, ZIP _____

Phone/Fax/E-mail _____

Notes _____

YOUR PROFESSIONAL NETWORK (continued)

Name _____

Position _____

Organization _____

Address _____

City, State, ZIP _____

Phone/Fax/E-mail _____

Notes _____

Name _____

Position _____

Organization _____

Address _____

City, State, ZIP _____

Phone/Fax/E-mail _____

Notes _____

Name _____

Position _____

Organization _____

Address _____

City, State, ZIP _____

Phone/Fax/E-mail _____

Notes _____

YOUR WORKLIFE NETWORK

Includes executive recruiters, college placement officers, career counselors. Can provide information, referrals, counseling.

Name _____

Position _____

Organization _____

Address _____

City, State, ZIP _____

Phone/Fax/E-mail _____

Notes _____

Name _____

Position _____

Organization _____

Address _____

City, State, ZIP _____

Phone/Fax/E-mail _____

Notes _____

Name _____

Position _____

Organization _____

Address _____

City, State, ZIP _____

Phone/Fax/E-mail _____

Notes _____

YOUR WORKLIFE NETWORK (continued)

Name _____

Position _____

Organization _____

Address _____

City, State, ZIP _____

Phone/Fax/E-mail _____

Notes _____

Name _____

Position _____

Organization _____

Address _____

City, State, ZIP _____

Phone/Fax/E-mail _____

Notes _____

Name _____

Position _____

Organization _____

Address _____

City, State, ZIP _____

Phone/Fax/E-mail _____

Notes _____

Name _____

Position _____

Organization _____

Address _____

City, State, ZIP _____

Phone/Fax/E-mail _____

Notes _____

WORKSHEETS

Writing Letters

Letters Worksheet 1

LETTER CONTENT ORGANIZER

Answer the following questions to organize the content of your letter. Then use your answer to compose the letter. Regarding a specific company, department, or need:

What is the problem or concern you might help solve? _____
_____
_____
_____

How can you assist the employer right away? _____
_____
_____
_____
_____

What have you accomplished that demonstrates your added value to this employer? _____
_____
_____
_____
_____

How will the employer specifically benefit from hiring you? _____

_____

_____

_____

LETTER DRAFT

(Your Address) _____

_____

_____

_____ (Date)

_____ (Name and Address)

_____

_____

Dear _____:
(Use a strong opening that gets right to the point.)

_____

_____

_____

(Demonstrate your knowledge of the employer and address ways you feel you can contribute to the employer's needs.)

_____

_____

_____

_____

(End your letter with a call to action. Ask for a meeting.)

_____

_____

_____

_____

Sincerely,

_____

Letters Worksheet 2

LETTER CONTENT ORGANIZER

Answer the following questions to organize the content of your letter. Then use your answer to compose the letter. Regarding a specific company, department, or need:

What is the problem or concern you might help solve? _____

_____

_____

_____

How can you assist the employer right away? _____

_____

_____

_____

What have you accomplished that demonstrates your added value to this employer? _____

_____

_____

_____

How will the employer specifically benefit from hiring you? _____

_____

_____

LETTER DRAFT

(Your Address) _____

_____

_____

_____ (Date)

_____ (Name and Address)

_____

_____

Dear _____:

(Use a strong opening that gets right to the point.)

_____

_____

_____

(Demonstrate your knowledge of the employer and address ways you feel you can contribute to the employer's needs.)

_____

_____

_____

_____

_____

_____

(End your letter with a call to action. Ask for a meeting.)

_____

_____

_____

_____

Sincerely,

_____

LETTER CONTENT ORGANIZER

Answer the following questions to organize the content of your letter. Then use your answer to compose the letter. Regarding a specific company, department, or need:

What is the problem or concern you might help solve? _____

_____

_____

_____

How can you assist the employer right away? _____

_____

_____

_____

_____

What have you accomplished that demonstrates your added value to this employer? _____

_____

_____

_____

_____

How will the employer specifically benefit from hiring you? _____

_____

_____

_____

_____

LETTER DRAFT

(Your Address) _____

_____

_____

_____ (Date)

_____ (Name and Address)

_____

_____

Dear _____:

(Use a strong opening that gets right to the point.)

_____

_____

_____

(Demonstrate your knowledge of the employer and address ways you feel you can contribute to the employer's needs.)

_____

_____

_____

_____

_____

_____

(End your letter with a call to action. Ask for a meeting.)

_____

_____

_____

_____

Sincerely,

_____

Letters Worksheet 4

LETTER CONTENT ORGANIZER

Answer the following questions to organize the content of your letter. Then use your answer to compose the letter. Regarding a specific company, department, or need:

What is the problem or concern you might help solve? _____

_____

_____

_____

How can you assist the employer right away? _____

_____

_____

_____

_____

What have you accomplished that demonstrates your added value to this employer? _____

_____

_____

_____

_____

How will the employer specifically benefit from hiring you? _____

_____

_____

_____

_____

LETTER DRAFT

(Your Address) _____

_____

_____

_____ (Date)

_____ (Name and Address)

_____

_____

Dear _____:
(Use a strong opening that gets right to the point.)

_____

_____

_____

(Demonstrate your knowledge of the employer and address ways you feel you can contribute to the employer's needs.)

_____

_____

_____

_____

_____

_____

(End your letter with a call to action. Ask for a meeting.)

_____

_____

_____

_____

Sincerely,

_____

SAMPLE PARAGRAPHS

Cover Letters

a. Opening Options

I saw the [_____] position as [posted/advertised] and would like to submit my resume for consideration. In my [____] years with [_____] in the [department] as a [_____], I've developed the qualities you need to meet your goals.

According to [internal contact/company newsletter, external contact], I understand that you are considering [goals, projects, direction] and may be in the market for someone who can provide strong leadership in pursuit of this goal.

The article in [company newsletter/external publication] about your [department/firm] was very impressive. Congratulations. I'm pleased to see you get recognition for your commitment to [_____] .

[Internal contact/external contact] suggested that since my background is in [_____], I get in touch with you to find out how I can best contribute to your [department's/company's] work in [_____].

I'm contacting [department heads, colleagues], such as yourself, to ask if you can offer any career opportunities in the [_____] area where a person with my [_____] skills, and my [____] years working for [_____] in the [department], could be valuable to supporting your efforts.

As an employee of [_____] in the [department], I'm well aware of your [department's/firm's] strong reputation in [_____] and [_____].

I have been following your [department's/company's] progress in [_____] for [____] years and believe that the skills I've developed while working at [_____] in the [department] the past [____] years will make a significant contribution to meeting your goals.

As I will be returning to school this fall to make myself a more valuable employee for [_____], I would like to apply for a part-time position, where I believe I can continue to be of value.

I saw the [notice posted/advertisement] for a part-time position as a [_____] and wish to express my interest and enthusiasm in transferring the [_____] skills I developed in my current position as a [_____] at [_____].

As a leader in the field, I admire your work in [_____]. I have been following your progress in [_____] for [_____] years.

I am moving to [_____], and I understand that your company is one of the area's leading firms in [_____] and [_____].

b. Body Options

I believe that with your [department's/firm's] reputation as a [_____], and my fresh insight into [_____], I could make a significant contribution right away.

With my background in [_____], I believe my unique skills would promote [the company's] continued growth and success.

If you need someone who can [_____], I believe I would make a noticeable difference [in your department/at your company].

Because I have [_____] years of experience in [_____], I thought you would be able to utilize my [_____] skills to help meet the needs of your [department/firm].

Since my background is in [_____], [internal contact/external contact] believes that I could be a valuable team player with your [department/company] right away.

I share your interest in [_____] and would like to offer my [_____] skills to match your need for a [_____].

Now that I have completed advanced [training/education] and received my [_____], I believe that in combination with my [_____] years as a [_____] at [_____], I can offer a more up-to-the-minute capability than ever to your [department/firm].

While my hourly commitment would not be full-time, the experience and skills in [_____] and [_____] that I can bring to the position will reflect my [_____] years in the field of [_____].

For the past [_____] years, I have worked as a [_____] with [department/company]. During this time, I have acquired experience in [_____] and earned recognition for [_____]. I am especially proud of [_____]. (*Add your unique selling points.*)

My involvement in [_____] has provided opportunities to practice the skills of [_____] and [_____]. I understand that these capabilities are important to a [department/firm] that excels in [_____]. (*Add your unique selling points.*)

In my career as a [_____], I have had the opportunity to hone my problem-solving skills. In particular, I've learned how to facilitate [_____] and [_____]. These abilities prove vital when I [_____]. (*Add your unique selling points.*)

As a [_____], I feel I have two unique benefits to offer: [_____] and [_____]. Throughout my career, these qualities have produced an increase in [_____]. They have also encouraged others to [_____]. (*Add your unique selling points.*)

I know that a [_____] has to have the quality of [_____], and I know that quality is important to your [department/firm]. It's a characteristic that I've worked on throughout my career. My [_____] and [_____] have produced consistent [_____]. (*Add your unique selling points.*)

Throughout my career, I have worked on my ability to [_____]. The results in [_____] have won acclaim from [_____] and [_____]. In particular, I am proud of the [_____] where I [_____]. (*Add your unique selling points.*)

In my experience with [_____], I've had to learn new [_____] and [_____] quickly but thoroughly. If training in [_____] and [_____] is necessary for success with your [department/company], then I'm ready. (*Add your unique selling points.*)

When I was [_____], I developed a successful [_____]. This important project brought my [department/company] a [_____] percent increase in sales. After studying your [department/firm], I feel that I could achieve similar results after a period of [_____]. (*Add your unique selling points.*)

Although it has been several years since I worked with [_____], I believe that my ability to [_____] and [_____] will prove valuable. The new opening sounds like a perfect opportunity to offer these skills as a [_____] [in your department/at your company]. (*Add your unique selling points*.)

My [_____] years of work in [_____] should be unique among your applicants. I feel my combination of [_____] skills and on-the-job experience is an ideal match for your needs. (*Add your unique selling points*.)

c. Closing Options

I am confident that my knowledge and abilities would be of value to your [department/company]. I would like to request a few minutes of your time to discuss my qualifications. I will contact you on [_____] to arrange a meeting. If you have any questions in the meantime, please do not hesitate to call.

Although I know your time is valuable, I would appreciate a few minutes to discuss my qualifications and how they might directly benefit your [department/organization]. I will contact you on [_____] to set up a meeting. Please do not hesitate to call if you have any questions.

Your commitment to [_____] and my willingness to [_____] look like a strong match. I'm sure this relationship will be good for the growth of [department/company]. I will contact you on [_____] to arrange a meeting to discuss the future possibilities. Please don't hesitate to contact me should you wish to reach me before this date.

I would appreciate a chance to meet with you and discuss how my skills could assist your [department/company] in its goal to [_____]. I will be in the area on [_____] and will call you on [_____] to see if there is a convenient time we can meet during my stay. If this time won't work for you, please don't hesitate to call me at [_____].

Interview Follow-up Letters

a. Opening Options

It was a pleasure to have met with you on [_____] regarding the opening you have in your [department/company] for a [_____].

Thank you for taking some of your valuable time to meet with me on [_____] about the [_____] position in your [department/firm]. During the interview, I learned that the qualities you need are a close match to the ones I've developed in my career at [_____].

Our personal meeting on [_____] regarding the [_____] position served to enlighten me further on the qualities your [department/company] desires in an employee.

Having met with you about the [_____] position on [_____], I feel that although our time together allowed me greater insight into the needs of your [department/organization], I was not able to give you the full scope of my ability to meet those needs. I would now like to take a few more minutes of your valuable time to do so.

Thank you for taking the time to meet with me about the [_____] position in your [department/company]. While I realize that the position is highly competitive, I would like to take just a moment more of your valuable time to review my unique skills and how they could directly benefit your [department/firm].

I so appreciate the time you spent on [_____] discussing the [_____] position with me. At the time, you had mentioned contacting me on [_____]. Because I understand how demanding your job must be, and I had not heard from you, I would like to take this opportunity to once again let you know what I can offer you in return for a position in your [department/company].

I would like to thank you for the opportunity to meet in person to discuss the [_____] position. As we met on [_____], and I have not yet heard from you, I wanted to let you know that I am still an interested candidate. Let me take just another minute of your time to review the unique skills I have to offer your [department/firm].

I am writing to follow up on the initial inquiry I wrote to you on [_____]. At the time, I forwarded you a cover letter and resume that highlighted my [_____] and [_____] in response to your [_____] opening.

b. Body Options

As we discussed during the interview, I believe my unique skills as a [_____] and a [_____] would promote your [department's/company's] continued growth and success.

I am convinced now more than ever that my contributions as a [_____] would add to the future success of your [department/company].

Again, I'd like to propose that with your [department's/firm's] reputation as a [_____], and my fresh insight into [_____], I would be of immediate value to you.

After our discussion, I was assured that with my [____] years of experience in [_____], you would be able to utilize my [_____] skills to help meet the needs of your [department/company].

During our interview, we discussed the [department's/company's] need for [_____] and [_____]. I'd like to take another moment of your valuable time to review the unique contributions I've been able to make while employed as a [_____] at [_____] in the [_____] department. (*Add your unique selling points.*) Given the opportunity to succeed in your [department/company], I believe I can offer the same results.

Having met with you in person, I am now better able to understand the skills your [department/company] seeks in an employee. If you review those skills against my own job history, you will see that I have developed the same skills you seek. As a [_____], I have demonstrated [_____] and [_____] qualities over a period of [____] years at [_____], and am most proud of [_____]. (*Add your unique selling points.*)

Once again, I'd like to highlight the unique benefits I have to offer as a [_____] in the [_____] field. During my [____] years in this field, I was able to [_____] and [_____]. I think the experiences I gained will be of immeasurable value to your [department/firm] should you decide to hire me as a [_____]. (*Add your unique selling points.*)

While we did not get much time during the interview to touch upon the [＿＿＿＿＿＿] skills I acquired as a [＿＿＿＿＿＿], in retrospect, I now think that these are the kinds of skills that are required for the job you described. When I was a [＿＿＿＿＿＿] in the [department/field], I was able to develop [＿＿＿＿＿＿] and [＿＿＿＿＿＿] to the satisfaction of my [manager/employer]. In particular, I am proud of the [＿＿＿＿＿＿] where I was able to [＿＿＿＿＿＿] for [＿＿＿＿＿＿]. (*Add your unique selling points.*)

c. Closing Options

Once again I'd like to thank you for meeting with me in person to discuss the [＿＿＿＿＿＿] opening. Because I hope that you will consider me as an active candidate, I will be calling back on [＿＿＿＿＿＿] to check on the status of your interview process. In the meantime, please feel free to call me at [＿＿＿＿＿＿] if you have any questions.

I sincerely appreciate the time you took to meet with me about the current opening in your [＿＿＿＿＿＿] department [at your company]. Please consider this letter as a sign of continued interest in offering your [department/company] the unique skills I've developed. I plan on checking back with your office in the next week to find out whether or not I'm still being considered. In the meantime, please feel free to call me should you seek references and/or recommendations.

SECTION THREE

RESUME CATALOG

THE *IMPERFECT* RESUME HALL OF FAME

100+ SAMPLES OF SOME OF OUR BEST
. . . AND OUR GOOD ENOUGH

Greetings to those of you starting this book right here. We know that people in a hurry will open up resume books and go right to the samples, find someone similar to themselves, and copy as much as possible. That's okay. There's good material here to steal.

However, we highly recommend you read the front of the book, just to understand our frame of reference. Then read many if not all of these samples, not just those in your past or future work category. There is much to learn from each of them.

All the samples come from real people, always disguised for their anonymity, and sometimes enhanced for our teaching purposes. And while these real people have applied the rules, they've occasionally broken them to make their message work. Mixed formating is allowed if it makes the resume read better.

All of the resumes are one-pagers. However, we know from experience how hard it is for many people with more than ten years' experience to write a one-page resume. Even professional writers find editing painful. So we edited some of our two-page originals to one page to provide the quickest punch. These resumes still deliver the essential message, only fat-free. Do your best to write simply and directly, even if you do end up with two pages.

You will not find a single "Career Objective" or "Summary of Qualifi-cations" at the top of our resume samples. We have never read even one of either of such statements that in any way enhanced or clarified what followed. Generally, these statements are as ineffective as standard, broadcast cover letters. Avoid writing either kind.

Additionally, almost 30 percent of our samples are in the targeted format. We know these are a challenge. To effectively write the capabili-ties, candidates need to have specific knowledge deriving from their direct experience, some additional research, and finally, an assertive attitude. Some of our samples, such as those prepared by new graduates, show an assertive attitude, but with minimal research and little direct experience. Nevertheless, the boldness of the targeted resume is impressive. It demon-strates focus and an entrepreneurial spirit, both desirable qualities in to-day's competitive job market.

Some of our resumes include statements that seem to be less power-ful than what we recommend. Other resumes are loaded with results and accomplishments. This is because some work lends itself easily to statistical documenting, while other work is by its very nature softer and fuzzier around the edges. Whenever possible, work should be described with specific outcomes. On the other hand, gratuitous self-praise, exaggerations, and outright lies are a no-no. They don't work.

You don't have to lie to write a good-enough resume. The only thing worse than writing a weaker but honest resume is writing a stronger but dishonest one. And the only thing worse than being caught in fudging the truth in an interview is being caught as incompetent on the job. You're right back to square one, only this time you've added shame and perhaps lost the job. You may even keep your job, but you've sent the message that you can't be trusted.

Remember the big picture: The best resumes are just one tool to get you the best interviews. The secrets to moving on or moving ahead in your worklife are in your self-knowledge, your interpersonal skills, your technical knowledge and practical experience, your openness to learning, and your willingness to risk yourself in a world of continuous change.

In the final analysis the best employment opportunities and the most effective job campaigns follow the courageous commitment to daily confront: No, No, No, No, No, No, No, No, No, No, No, No . . . *Yes!*

To get to your goals sooner, collect more Nos faster! "Horray! I got six nos today! Only seventy-three more to go!"

Most overnight success happens over weeks, months, or even years.

Write on your refrigerator: **Winners never quit and quitters never win.** And then type up one hundred Nos and paste them under your winners quote. Count them and cross them off as you collect them. Your Nos are the measure of your success.

RESUME INDEX BY OCCUPATIONAL CATEGORY

MARY LOWE
22 Harp Court
Morristown, NJ 07960
(201) 555-2379

MANAGEMENT AND SUPERVISION

- Administered telephone switched-access capacity management for Massachusetts, Hartford (CT) and Newburgh (NY), including current trunk usage, grade of service requirements, and correction of potential servicing problems.

- Managed AT&T International Operating Center and maintained responsibility for all international results, labor relations, all union and nonunion personnel issues, and international customer relations.

- Managed Relocation Benefits Department including home-sale plans, homes-in-inventory, and the implementation of domestic and international moving plans.

- Supervised regional implementation of Performance/Attendance Improvement Program for 17,000 participants.

PROGRAM DEVELOPMENT AND TRAINING

- Designed information packets, audiovisual materials, seminars and face-to-face communication program for relocating employees utilizing multimedia and scheduling software.

- Established spouse counseling program to assist trailing spouse in finding new employment.

- Represented AT&T as speaker and panel member at relocation seminars.

- Introduced new ideas to assist relocating employees through home buyers' counseling service, videotapes of communities and homes, and customized town profile reports.

- Developed and presented seminars for 1200 employees including internal and external coordination for salary administration, pension calculation, predecision counseling, and outplacement.

WORK HISTORY

1964 - Present	AT&T: Basking Ridge, NJ
1996 - Present	Supervisor, Access Engineering
1993 - 1996	Manager, Relocation Benefits and Pioneers
1987 - 1993	Staff Supervisor, Relocation Benefits and Pioneers

EDUCATION/PROFESSIONAL AFFILIATIONS

- AT&T Training Center: Professional Development Seminars
- Manhattanville College, Pace University, Kings College Intern Program

GERRI BADNER

321 Central Park West #5-A
New York, NY 10025
(212) 555-7760 FAX (212) 555-7767

PROJECT COORDINATION

- Managed and coordinated the packaging concept and layout of an entire computer software package, including artwork concepts, graphic design and color choices.
- Worked with production and distribution vendors for software product.
- Arranged full logistics for company participation in quarterly trade shows.
- Proficient with Lotus Notes and video conferencing software.
- Provided liaison between Paris and New York, handling foreign exchange problems, travel, and other international trade issues.
- Assisted in setup, administration, accounting, bookkeeping, and advertising.

RETAIL ADMINISTRATION

- Assisted in setting up and hanging photography gallery exhibits.
- Organized and inventoried photographs using Microsoft Access.
- Worked extensively with clients on the phone and in person.
- Handled, showed, and sold works of art.
- Organized mailing lists, books, and artists' biographies.
- Aided in artistic choice decisions for advertising and American product design.

SPECIAL SKILLS

- Fluent in written and oral French.
- Operate movie cameras and direct short-subject stories.

WORK HISTORY

1996 - Present
FRN INTERNATIONAL: New York, NY
Business Manager

1995
HOWARD HARTMANN, INC.: New York, NY
Assistant to Gallery Owner

1993 - 1995
SOFT-THINK SYSTEMS, INC.: New York, NY
Special Projects Coordinator

EDUCATION

1993
VASSAR COLLEGE: Poughkeepsie, NY
B.A. in Language and Literature - Photography Minor

1991
INSTITUT DE FRANCAIS: Paris, France
French Language and Art History

JOANNE B. HOWARD

723 Merrill Avenue
Peekskill, NY 10776
(914) 555-7766 Messages   Compuserve: 68954,3142

WORK HISTORY

1992 - Present   CRESTLINE COMMUNICATIONS: Pleasantville, NY

                      Program Manager
                      Manage a customer service/marketing program targeting the company's
                      top customers nationally, resulting in $437,000 sales per year. Identify
                      opportunities, formulate strategies, and implement plans to stimulate
                      sales of company's microcomputer software product line. Supervise
                      staff of six.

1986 - 1992   GROUP HEALTH ASSOCIATES: Seattle, WA

   1992   Administrative Analyst II
                      Developed decision papers for trustees and executives of $360 million
                      budget HMO. Identified organizational impact of issues and
                      recommended alternative options. Edited managerial materials for
                      presentation to board, consulting with senior level executives in the
                      development of information.

   1986 - 1991   Assistant Office Director
                      Supervised staff of six. Oversaw transition of office to fully automated
                      office system, resulting in increased staff productivity and higher
                      morale. Wrote newsletters and speeches for trustees. Developed and
                      refined a computerized data base management program, improving the
                      speed in retrieving information used in decision-making. Managed a
                      reduction in staff due to organizational budget cuts, maintaining
                      productivity standard with fewer staff members.

1985 - 1986   AMERICAN ASSOCIATION OF RETIRED PERSONS
                      Washington, DC

                      Legislative Specialist
                      Researched, analyzed, and reported legislative interests of association's
                      membership. Organized association's first formal legislative
                      correspondence section, improving response time to over 500 letters
                      received each month.

EDUCATION

1992   UNIVERSITY OF WASHINGTON: Seattle, WA
                      Master of Public Administration

1982   ELMIRA COLLEGE: Elmira, NY
                      B.A., Political Science, cum laude

MARK HARGROVE

55 Sherwood Street
Wildwood, NJ 07886
Home: (201) 555-6572   Work: (201) 555-2000, ext. 3938

WORK EXPERIENCE

1986 - Present   ARCO MINING & ALLOYS COMPANY: Secaucus, NJ

1990 - Present   Manager, Chemicals Procurement

Manage a corporate procurement group that purchases the major
chemical raw materials for over 100 consuming plants in the U.S.
Commodity responsibility includes pulp and paper chemicals, plastic
resins, inks, waxes, coatings, solvents, plastic film and sheet, and
lignosulfonates. Direct six professional buyers and nonexempt
programs saving over $1MM per year. Initiated program in support of
Hazardous Waste Disposal project. Participated in strategy planning
and negotiations for key raw materials.

1986 - 1990˙   Materials Manager

Designed and implemented necessary systems and procedures to
establish purchasing activities between corporate purchasing and
AM&A.

1981 - 1986   CHEMICALS & PHARMACEUTICALS, LTD.: Secaucus, NJ

Purchasing Agent

Negotiated for approximately $40MM of specialty and commodity raw
materials. Contributed significantly to C and P's cost reduction
program. Performed liaison function between corporate purchasing and
Allied of Canada, Ltd. Implemented program to improve reporting
systems between plants and purchasing.

1977 - 1981   TECHNIKON CHEMICAL CORPORATION: Union, NJ

Technical Specialist II

Performed research, development, and scale-up on advanced aerospace
polymers. Invented seven materials for which patents were awarded.

EDUCATION

Various management courses sponsored by Arco Mining & Alloys Co.,
and Chemicals & Pharmaceuticals, Ltd.

Upsala College: Lindhurst, NJ
Chemistry and Business

MAURA SHANDLING
22 Carriage Lane
Saddle River, NJ 07458
(201) 555-5276 Fax (201) 555-5878

1989 - Present	BIERBAUM & SONS, NEW JERSEY DIVISION: 26 Midwest stores headquarters - Paramus, NJ
1992 - Present	Merchandise Counselor Men's Dress Shirts

Senior merchandising executive reporting to Group Vice-President, supervising four buyers.

Work closely with international designers and manufacturers in London, Paris, Milan, Hong Kong and Singapore. Increased sales volume 150%: $8M to $20M with a 216% increase in profit. Changed product mix through analysis of merchandise productivity and profitability. Developed new product-line vendor relations and negotiations resulting in higher profit margins. Designed and oversaw in-store merchandising plans for all stores. Redirected inventory standards resulting in reduced shortages. Provided effective training for store personnel resulting in increased sales and team spirit.

1992	Store Merchandise Manager Sportswear, Juniors, Dresses, Coats, Furniture, Housewares and Domestics

Increased volume 25%: $15M to $20M compared to total store increase of 15%. Directed total concept thinking. Analyzed business and maximized sales through improved merchandise acquisition, elimination of slow selling merchandise, optimal floor plans and effective training.

1989 - 1992	Buyer Updated Sportswear, Handbags, Misses Sportswear, Maternity Wear

Escalated sales from $4M to $9M and profit from -25% to +10% within one year (Updated Sportswear). Enhanced product development through international travel and exploration (Updated Sportswear). Developed volume from $2M to $3.5M and profit reflecting a 70% increase (Handbags). Operated highly successful import program; traveled extensively to Hong Kong, Korea, Manila, and Europe (Handbags). Directed volume increase of 30% from $2.3 to $3M producing a 43% profit increase (Misses Sportswear). Augmented annual volume 40% from $1M to $1.4M, producing a 43% profit increase (Maternity Wear).

EDUCATION

St. John's University
B.S. - Commerce/Marketing

JO BETH SHOWALTER

336 Ardsley Place
Birmingham, AL 35209
(203) 555-5612

RESTAURANT MANAGEMENT

- Established total front house system of a 300-seat business. Directed all hiring, training, motivating, and scheduling of 15-person staff. Handled payroll. Managed liquor and food orders and all inventory control.
- Interfaced with corporate clientele, successfully building strong relationships and repeat business. Directed unique setup of three kitchens, with three separate sets of chefs. Became restaurant's first female manager and handled all operations with equal ease.

INSTRUCTION / TEACHING

- Established art program, designing progressive curriculum for grades 1-8. Successfully taught youngsters of all abilities.
- Taught English and speech, and managed drama program for several hundred students.
- Designed and implemented a highly successful dropout prevention program for underprivileged students resulting in a dramatic shift in self-esteem, retention in school, and eventual decision to enter careers with a future.

THEATRICAL MANAGEMENT

- Managed the professional careers of two children which included TV, commercials, movies and Broadway. 1987-1990
- Assisted in children's productions with the Capron Studios, a Children's Theater Workshop; handled coaching, staging, and costuming. 1985-1988

EXPERIENCE

1992 - 1996   HOULIHAN'S RESTAURANT & PUB: Birmingham, AL
General Manager

1991 - 1992   YAMIYURI JAPANESE RESTAURANT: Birmingham, AL
Day Manager

1984 - 1990   ST. AGNES SCHOOL: Montgomery, AL
Teacher

EDUCATION

University of Alabama
One course to Master's Degree - Theatre and Communications

Sanford College
B.A. - English/Art

JASON S. ALEXANDER
2668 Lanhart Road
Little Rock, AR 72204
(501) 555-8824   AOL-ALEXARK

JOB TARGET

MANAGEMENT TRAINEE, MATERIALS MANAGEMENT

CAPABILITIES

- Interview vendors to obtain product information, pricing and delivery date.
- Discuss defects of goods with quality control or inspection personnel to determine source of trouble and take corrective actions.
- Keep computerized records pertaining to inventory, costs, and deliveries.
- Make sound decisions based on personal experience and judgment as well as verifiable facts and data.
- Work long hours without physical stress or annoyance.

ACCOMPLISHMENTS

- Supervised and coordinated trucking terminal workers' activities and assignments in distribution and loading of goods.
- Inspected shipments for damage, and trained dock workers in correct ways to handle different kinds of material. Achieved monthly awards for one year straight.
- Processed and handled billing documents.
- Handled customer complaints by determining freight location and estimating time of delivery using nationwide IBM communications system. Cut errors by 40%.
- Located and expedited rush shipments.

WORK HISTORY

1994 - present   Operations Coordinator
                  HOLLIS TRUCK LINES, INC.: Little Rock, AR

1990 - 1994   Office Help/Laborer
                  WOODLEY CONSTRUCTION COMPANY: Little Rock, AR

EDUCATION

1994   University of Arkansas
                  B.S. - Policy and Administration

TAYLOR E. WHITTAKER
12 Beyer Court
Rhinebeck, New York 11293
(914) 555-4480 COMPUSERVE 67999.2403

TARGET   OUTSOURCED EMPLOYEE BENEFITS MANAGING

CAPABILITIES
- Direct a comprehensive employee benefits program for up to 30,000 employees.
- Negotiate contracts with insurance and other benefits personnel.
- Manage labor relations negotiations and pre-negotiating planning.
- Analyze health-care programs for cost-effectiveness.
- Research both salaried and hourly benefits programs.
- Closely monitor federal, state, and local legislation and identify potential labor problems.
- Accurately and clearly communicate benefits programs details to both employer and employees.

ACHIEVEMENTS
- Developed employee benefits programs for over 250 hourly employees.
- Negotiated benefits contracts resulting in 17% savings on premiums.
- Identified potential problems in new legislation, avoiding several potentially costly lawsuits.
- Directed research on major new medical benefits program.
- Set cost-control standards which have since been adopted throughout pump industry.
- Developed new kit for use in communicating benefits program to hourly employees.

WORK HISTORY

1988 - 1996   BOSTON GEAR INTERNATIONAL: White Plains, NY
Labor Relations Manager

1984 - 1988   GENERAL MERCHANDISING CORP.: Stamford, CT
Personnel Administrator

1981 - 1984   UNITED PUMP MANUFACTURING: Stamford, CT
Assistant Personnel Manager

1980 - 1981   Employment Counselor

EDUCATION

1981   FORDHAM UNIVERSITY: New York, NY
B.A. - Liberal Arts

FELICIA DOWNING SINGLETON
115 Swanner Place
Salt Lake City, UT 84401
(801) 555-8802, AOL DOWNSING

1989 - 1996	WORLDWIDE DYNAMICS (WD) COMPANY
1993 - 1996	CORPORATE RESEARCH & DEVELOPMENT CTR.: Albany, NY
1994 - 1996	Manager, Employee Relations Programs Provided comprehensive employee relations support to approximately 1,000 technical and professional employees. Introduced and managed new career development training program for employees. Administered annual manpower review. Supervised eight employees.
1993 - 1994	Administrator, Organization and Staffing Administered annual manpower and staffing review. Developed management candidates' slates. Designed programs with local schools to enhance science and math education.
1989 - 1993	FARMINGTON ATOMIC POWER RESEARCH LAB: Troy, NY
1992 - 1993	Supervisor, Professional Recruiting Hired 160 engineers and scientists. Coordinated campus visits for 60 WD recruiters. Completed U.S. Government audit of recruiting practices with successful outcome. Supervised five employees.
1991 - 1992	Specialist, Education and Training Managed $1/2 million budget. Administered technical and non-technical training programs for laboratory personnel. Provided career counseling to employees.
1989 - 1991	Specialist, Recruitment and Placement Sourced, recruited, hired, and oriented new technical employees.
1986 - 1989	LANGELY TECHNICAL INSTITUTE: Schenectady, NY Assistant Director, Financial Aid Completed needs analyses. Awarded aid packages. Counseled students and parents regarding eligibility. Responded to problem correspondence for Director and President.

EDUCATION

1986	State University of New York: New Paltz, NY M.S. - Personnel and Counseling
1984	State University of New York: Binghamton, NY B.S. - Psychology and Elementary Education

JAMES BURROUGHS
31 Purple Sage Road
Houston, TX 77049
Home: (703) 555-5572 Office: 555-1264 Fax: 555-1265

WORK HISTORY:

1985 - Present	Westfield Chemical Company (WCC): Houston, Texas
1992 - 1994	Westfield Photo Division Company (WPD): Atlanta, Georgia

1994 - Present   Quality Management Consultant
WCC
Consultant for both WCC's Administrative Organization Redesign process and strategic intent initiative. Maintained full responsibility for developing and implementing plans/courses of action for several management and technical teams.

1992 - 1994   Original Westfield Photo Quality Core Team Member
Original member responsible for initiating and leading the WP Quality Leadership Process in two of the largest business units, three major support organizations and the Latin American region impacting close to 3000 employees. In addition, developed an infrastructure of internal consultants through training and consultation.

1990 - 1992   Pilot of Team Management - Textile Fibers Division
Coordinator of entire Team Management effort with full responsibility for seventy interlocking teams. As a design team member, pioneered planning, implementing, and coaching facets of the quality process.

1985 - 1990   Project Industrial Engineer and Systems Analyst

EDUCATION:

1985   B.S. - Industrial Engineering/Operations Research
Texas A & M University

SUPPORTING DATA:

Formal Quality Training, Swarthborne Institute: Quality Management/Leadership Process; Team Management Consultant Training; Performance Management; Decision-Making Styles; Listening Skills; Deming Philosophy; Statistical Methods; Problem Solving and Group Dynamics.

PROFESSIONAL AFFILIATIONS:

Institute of Industrial Engineers; have served in all officer capacities. American Society of Quality Control; maintain active role in local chapter.

SALLYANNE CARTWRIGHT
44 Washington Avenue #2B
Reston, VA 44011
(703) 555-9833, Fax (703) 555-9820

WORK HISTORY

1983 - present   BLUERIDGE PRODUCTS, INC.: Alexandria, VA

1992 - present   **National Sales Manager**

Managed $45 million of sales for food service and bakery
company exceeding sales targets in both pounds and units.
Increased profits 45% in last fiscal year. Managed 13 sales
managers and 45 brokers nationally. Completely overhauled
customer service department resulting in stronger
communications between units. Conceived and implemented
methods for substantially reducing unabsorbed freight and
bringing $11,000 per month to the bottom line.

1989 - 1992   **Sales Manager** - Food Service Division

Responsible for 75% of annual corporate sales. Launched
new line as major marketing need for deli department in
supermarket trade; added new products to fit in line.
Instituted use of outside manufacturing sources to improve
profitability of marginal products.

1983 - 1989   **Eastern Divisional Manager**

Headed five east coast food service and bakery territories
providing $25 million in annual sales; increased sales
volume by 35%. Trained field regional managers and
brokers. Dropped unprofitable direct retail sales division and
incorporated into master distributor program.

EDUCATION

1991   GEORGE MASON UNIVERSITY: Fairfax, VA
M.B.A.

1983   GEORGE MASON UNIVERSITY: Fairfax, VA
B.A. - English and History

MARGARET SILVER
El Camino Real
Palo Alto, CA 94306
(415) 555-3367 - days (415) 555-8824 - eves

JOB TARGET: TELECOMMUNICATIONS CONSULTING MANAGER

CAPABILITIES:

- Manage significant amounts of annual revenue.
- Provide telecommunications management, sales, design, and implementation functions on the job.
- Effectively communicate and provide interpersonal skills with all levels of business customers and management.
- Manage details under pressure in complex and competitive environments.

ACCOMPLISHMENTS:

- Managed $6.5 million of Pacific Bell revenue.
- Maintained 120% of annual objective in 1991, 1993, 1994, and 1995.
- Managed 110 new business customers to maximize their market share.
- Received outstanding sales award for creating $1.5 million in new revenue.

EXPERIENCE:

1986 - Present	PACIFIC BELL TELEPHONE COMPANY: Burlingame, CA
1989 - Present	Account Executive BELL COMMUNICATION SYSTEMS
1986 - 1989	Customer Sales Representative System Design and Implementation
1984 - 1986	Store Manager THOMPSON'S GIFTS: Palo Alto, CA
1981 - 1984	Department Manager LIEBERMAN'S: Menlo Park, CA

EDUCATION:

Over 20 Pacific Bell technical and management training courses

San Francisco State College
B.S. - Business/Marketing

CAROL DAVISON
566 Maitland Avenue
Teaneck, NJ 07666
(201) 555-7755 - phone & fax   (212) 555-6700 - service

TELEVISION

Produced and directed the following video productions: "The Art of Batiking," "The Impossible Dream," "The Creative Process," and "Wildlife Conservation." Organized all aspects: scriptwriting; audio selection and placement; set design (including furniture building cards); and planning camera shots, angles, and composition.

FILM

Produced and directed the following: "Everybody Is a Star" and "Love Is a Beautiful Thing." Developed a 20-minute documentary: handled interviewing, narration, editing and all graphics.

RADIO

Produced a tape demonstrating special effects including echo, reverberations, and speed distortion.

TECHNICAL SKILLS

Can operate:
TV - studio cameras, Porta-Paks, Handycams, and switching panel.
FILM - various super 8mm cameras, viewers, splicers, and 16mm projectors.
RADIO - audio console, turntables, various tape machines; handle cueing and mixing.

EDUCATION

1993   NORTHEASTERN UNIVERSITY

                B.S. - Broadcasting and Film

1991   F.C.C. - Third Class Operator Permit

                Handled camera work, editing, splicing, lighting, and soundtrack. Designed and produced splicing, and final taping.

JESSICA HIGGINS
3422 Autumn Avenue
Brooklyn Heights, NY 11208
(718) 555-4451   AOL JESS99

CREATIVITY/DESIGN
- Developed programs in arts of the Middle Ages, history of food and gardening.
- Designed decoration materials for culinary exhibition.
- Developed themes for public festivals.
- Wrote and produced performing arts activities.
- Wrote scripts for special events at historical sites, museums and botanical gardens.
- Developed public information materials.
- Designed decorations, including floral, for special activities.

ORGANIZATION/PLANNING
- Organized art exhibitions.
- Researched and established formal garden tours.
- Planned and coordinated performing arts activities.
- Oversaw preparation of food for daily activities and special events.
- Organized New York University's Annual Alumni Day activities.
- Scheduled and coordinated various aspects involved in successful production of parties, special events, performances and festivals.
- Planned and developed itineraries for visiting scholars.

MANAGEMENT CONSULTING
- Advised employers and clients on protocol and etiquette.
- Provided support and advice on image at national women's convention.
- Assisted with implementation of Image Consultant's training programs.
- Provided special education in history, museums, dance, and theater.
- Managed popular New York restaurant and catering establishment.
- Managed, planned and coordinated special catering events, including the opening of the Mellon Wing at the National Gallery.

WORK HISTORY
1993 - Present   Senior Research Clerk
                     New York University: New York, NY

1988 - Present   Assistant to Director/Executive Board Member
                     Medieval Arts Council: New York, NY

1987 - 1988   Teacher
                     New York City Board of Education: New York, NY

1979 - 1985   Chef-Manager-Caterer
                     La Petite Minceur: Brooklyn Heights, NY

EDUCATION
1996   Columbia University, M.S. - Education
1990   Barnard College Graduate Program - Medieval History
1987   Columbia University, B.A. - Philosophy
1979   Madeline Senese's Modern Gourmet Cooking School: Chef's Diploma
           Special training in image and presentation - Images Consulting
           International

AARON I. WILSON
531 Olive Street
Smithtown, NY 11829
(516) 555-9531

JOB TARGET   Architect for a private firm.

CAPABILITIES

- Provide professional services in research, development, and design of large building complexes using CAD software
- Design alterations and renovations of many styles of architecture
- Fully design large fast food facilities, adaptable to many locales
- Design libraries with special consideration to sound and lighting
- Design shopping centers, particularly in semitropical climates
- Design drive-in and walk-in banks
- Design hospital and rest home facilities conforming to full health and safety standards

ACCOMPLISHMENTS

- Designed and constructed all county buildings and alterations thereto.
- Planned, organized, directed, and reviewed all architectural and engineering functions of my department's jurisdiction.
- Designed office buildings, data processing facilities, health centers, courts, police stations, power plants, access roads, and other facilities.
- Produced schematics, feasibility studies, reports, and cost estimates.
- Designed schools, libraries, and rest homes.

WORK HISTORY

1987 - Present   NASSAU COUNTY DEPT. OF BUILDINGS AND GROUNDS: Nassau, NY
County Architect

1980 - 1987   CARL N. TYNE & ASSOCIATES: Westbury, NY
Associate Architect

EDUCATION

1980   Nassau County Community College
State of New York Architecture License

AFFILIATIONS

- Corporate member - A.I.A.
- Member - New York State Association of Architects

ELIZA CASTLEBERRY
269 Mountain Place
Burlington, VT 05401
(802) 555-6700 - Service

STATISTICS

- Height: 5 feet 6 inches; Weight: 115; Eyes: Green; Hair: Auburn;
  D.O.B.: 4/4/74

SELECTED PERFORMING ARTS ACCOMPLISHMENTS

- "Miss Firecracker Contest" (Stage Play/Comedy) - Lead Role, Jarnelle, Burlington
  Group Theater, Ford Fine Arts Center, 1995
- "The Diary of Anne Frank" (Stage Play/Drama) - Mrs. Van Daan, St. Matthew's
  Academy Theater, Burlington, VT, 1992
- "The Ugly Duckling" (Stage Play/Fantasy) - Lead Role, Princess Camilla, St.
  Matthew's Academy Theater, Burlington, VT, 1991
- "Showdown at the Rainbow Ranch" (Stage Play/Melodrama) - Lead Role,
  Rainbow, New England Regional Theater, Manchester, NH, 1990
- "Teen" (Pop Rock Musical) - Lead Role, Mary, Marshall High School,
  Burlington, VT, 1990

SPECIAL TALENTS AND ACHIEVEMENTS

- Local/Regional/State Superior Awards - Duet Memorized Acting (Without Props)
- Eight Years Experience: Talents Shows (Musician/Singer/Actress)
- Musician: Guitar, Synthesizer, Piano, Saxophone, Clarinet
- Guitar/Vocal Training from Recording Artist/Professional Music Teachers
- Indian/Tap/Jazz Dancing; Horseback Riding (Both Saddle and Bareback)
- Write/Speak French and Hindi Languages
- Dialects Include: Southern/Eastern/Western; British/French Accents

MODELING/BEAUTY PAGEANTS

- Coordinator and Model for Several Fashion Shows in Local Area
- Junior Miss Pageant Overall 1st Runner-Up Award Winner
- Junior Miss Pageant: Talent, Physical Fitness, and Modeling Awards
- Miss Vermont Lovely Lady Pageant, Overall 1st Runner-Up Award Winner, 1989

SCHOOL PERFORMING ARTS EXPERIENCE

- Vermont Representative - Celebration Choir, Philadelphia, PA
- All-State/Tri-States Choir Member (Soprano); President, H.S. Choir
- Captain, Cheerleaders Squad; Drill Team Top Award Winner

EDUCATION

1992 - 1994 University of Vermont: Burlington, VT
Dual Major: Performing Arts/Broadcast Journalism

Courses: Acting, Music Appreciation, History of Rock and Roll
Editor, Newsletter for Campus Drama Group

ANGELA UNDERHILL
221 West University Parkway
Baltimore, MD 21210
(301) 555-9844 AOL FALCON

PHOTOGRAPHY

- As staff photographer for a magazine, designed setups for and photographed food products.
- Covered trade convention personnel and equipment.
- Photographed restaurant interior and institutional equipment.
- Illustrated articles on interior decoration.
- Shot outdoor scenics and nature close-ups.
- Photographed "how-to" series on construction projects, food preparation, and maintenance.
- Taught basic photography to sales staff.

WRITING

- Researched and wrote scientific articles in fields of chemistry, mathematics, and physics.
- Converted scientific data into lay terms.
- Researched and developed articles on industrial equipment, plastics, and food service.
- Wrote instruction manuals on data processing procedures.

EDITING

- Edited technical and semi-technical manuscripts in science field.
- Solicited authors for technical articles. Edited trade magazine copy.
- Made layouts and dummied pages. Freelance edited science books.

EMPLOYERS

1992 - 1996	GARBIER, INC.: Miami, FL Executive Assistant
1986 - 1992	EDIFICE MAGAZINE: Baltimore, MD Staff Photographer/Assistant Editor
1985 - 1986	MIAMI ACADEMY OF SCIENCES: Miami, FL Associate Editor

EDUCATION

Maryland Institute of Art
Non-credit courses in painting

Miami University
B.A. - English

KRIS PETERSEN
111 Fifth Avenue
New York City, NY 10006
h (212) 555-3326 w (212) 555-4511

PASTE-UP/MECHANICALS, GRAPHIC DESIGN

- Produced paste-ups and mechanicals for the weekly "close" of Newsday magazine.
- Designed brochures, booklists, using Print Shop Deluxe; selected type, conceptualized and produced monthly silk-screen posters.
- Planned displays for major metropolitan library.

TECHNICAL ILLUSTRATION/FORMS DESIGNER

- Mastered "LeRoy" lettering technique and created technical illustrations for research publication in the Photo-optics Department at SUNY - Buffalo.

FREE-LANCE DRAWING BOARD ARTIST/PHOTOGRAPHER

- Interfaced between client and printer from the drawing board in a commercial printing shop.
- Produced numerous printed materials, from business cards to annual reports, utilizing Freelance and Canvas.
- Supervised typesetter.
- Supervised a commercial photographic studio.
- Undertook diverse freelance jobs, including producing a 3' x 5' map of the State University campus, large lettering assignments, portrait and product photography for private individuals, and slide shows for a hospital and the University.

EXPERIENCE

1994 - Present	Free-Lance Artist
1989 - 1994	STATE UNIVERSITY OF NEW YORK: Buffalo, NY
1990	LEN KOCH, INC. (commercial printing): Smithtown, NY
1987 - 1989	BUFFALO PUBLIC LIBRARY: Buffalo, NY
1986 - 1987	NEWSDAY, INC.: Chicago, IL

EDUCATION

1990	THE SCHOOL OF VISUAL ARTS: New York, NY Commercial / Fine Arts
1986	UNIVERSITY OF CHICAGO B.A. - General Studies

NICOLE S. GARRIST

331 Cliff Court
Portland, OR 97208
(503) 555-9890; COMPUSERVE - COLGAR

INSURANCE LAW:

- Advised management of insurance company on legality of insurance transactions.
- Studied court decisions and recommended changes in wording of insurance policies to conform with law and/or to protect company from unwarranted claims.
- Advised claims department personnel of legality of claims filed on company to insure against undue payments.
- Advised personnel engaged in drawing up of legal documents such as insurance contracts and release papers.

CORPORATE LAW:

- Extensively studied corporation structure, including legal rights, obligations and privileges.
- Acted as agent for several corporations in various transactions.
- Studied decisions, statutes, and ordinances of quasi-judicial bodies.

REAL ESTATE LAW:

- Handled sale and transfer of real property.
- Instituted title searches to establish ownership.
- Drew up deeds, mortgages, and leases.
- Acted as trustee of property and held funds for investment.

WORK EXPERIENCE:

1988 - Present   COMMERCIAL AUTOMOBILE UNDERWRITERS
COMPANY, INC.: Portland, OR
Insurance Services Office Supervisor

EDUCATION:

1991   UNIVERSITY OF OREGON LAW SHOOL
LLB - Insurance Law

1988   UNIVERSITY OF OREGON
B.A. - History

JULIET MARIA THATCHER
269 West End Avenue, Apt. 57
New York, NY 10023
(212) 555-2311 - phone and fax

LITIGATION

Attained numerous credits in all phases of civil litigation in state and federal courts. Successfully conducted depositions and trials in a variety of media and commercial cases. Achieved notable results through expertise in state and federal court brief-writing. Reduced costs through self-training and management of department in creditors' rights and bankruptcy cases. Achieved favorable resolution of complex, difficult-to-win cases through meticulous work and deployment of group-supported strategies. Practiced before administrative boards and arbitrators.

MEDIA

Practiced in all aspects of media law for large and medium-sized clients. Conducted and directed media litigations with expertise. Avoided litigation through creative merging of legal and editorial skills in pre-publishing libel and privacy counseling. Analyzed and managed copyright and corporate matters. Planned and negotiated contracts and settlements.

MANAGEMENT

Skilled in perceptive direction of research, planning of trial and pre-trial strategy. Reduced unnecessary time spent by others on work projects through careful supervision of work. Maintained extensive client contact. Selected, supervised, and controlled local counsel in out-of-state cases to assure highest results while avoiding large billings.

EMPLOYMENT HISTORY

1992 - 1997   BALMER, KAYE, SOAMS, & HARTING: New York, NY
Senior Associate (1995-1997); Junior Associate (1992-1995)

EDUCATION

1992   COLUMBIA LAW SCHOOL
LLB, Cum Laude; Harlan Fiske Stone Scholar; Dean's List.

1988   COLUMBIA COLLEGE
B.A.; top 10% of class; Dean's List.

PUBLICATIONS

- *Columbia Journal of Law and Social Problems* - Editor
- *Kings Crown Essays* - Managing Editor

SUZANNE R. LURMAN
213 Sommerset Avenue
Minneapolis, MN 55042
(612) 555-8213

JOB TARGET   ACCOUNTING DEPARTMENT MANAGER

CAPABILITIES

- Manage large groups of people with ease.
- Analyze vast amounts of data into relevant financial statistics.
- Perform detailed customer audits.
- Develop systems and procedures for all phases of accounting.
- Utilize automated accounting system to produce monthly and yearly financial statements.
- Utilize pc/Lotus/advanced spreadsheets and train others.

ACCOMPLISHMENTS

- Conducted detailed audits of clients, saving senior accountants time.
- Devised specific computer programs for auditing use.
- Supervised daily data input of 27 person accounting department.
- Researched a detailed marketing study; helped refocus annual marketing plan.
- Administered all trustee-related aspects of bankruptcy proceedings, delivering findings in record time.
- Handled credit analyses and references and made credit recommendations.
- Installed and supervised automated payroll system, saving company tens of thousands.

WORK EXPERIENCE

1990 - Present   KARPSTER & HALBRAND, INC.: Minneapolis, MN
                   Staff B Accountant

1986 - 1989   BARNARD COLLEGE: New York, NY
                   Administrative Assistant

1983 - 1986   OSTERBERG, SHINDLER, & HART, P.C.: New York, NY
                   Paraprofessional in Bankruptcy

EDUCATION

1993   UNIVERSITY OF MINNESOTA, Graduate School of Business
                   MBA - Accounting

1983   BARNARD COLLEGE
                   B.A. - History

SULANI D. MURALSIKH

3345 Boulevard East, Apt. 145
West New York, NJ 07190
Home: (201) 555-5587 Office: (212) 555-3000, ext 59
Muralk@SMK.COM

WORK EXPERIENCE

1990 - Present   FEDERAL RESERVE BANK OF NEW YORK: New York, NY
                      Operations Analyst

Responsible for: developing proposals to top management for operational reviews;
organizing and managing the task forces to conduct the reviews; documenting and
presenting recommendations to top management; coordinating this bank's efforts with
similar initiatives in the Federal Reserve System.

1988 - 1990   UNITED NATIONS DEVELOPMENT PROGRAM: New York, NY
                     Planning Officer

Responsible for program planning, resource allocation, and evaluation of a $100 million
program of technical and capital assistance to developing countries in the area of
population control and economic development.

ACCOMPLISHMENTS

- Initiated, systematized, and managed a review of bank examinations and bank
  applications processing activities, resulting in annual savings of $1,500,000.
- Developed long-range plan, necessary capital, and operating budgets for the 185-
  person International Services Department; analyzed costs of foreign exchange and
  investment transactions.
- Organized and supervised a ten-month, fifteen-person study of the world contraceptive
  market, sponsored jointly by UNDP and the Ford Foundation.
- Developed a model-based forecasting system for program planning, management, and
  control.
- Developed population control projects for countries in East Africa and the Middle
  East.

EDUCATION

1992   New York University, Graduate School of Business
            Ph.D. - International Banking

1988   Massachusetts Institute of Technology
            M.S. - Management

            Rutgers University   B.S. - Physics

CHRIS ADAMSON DUNCAN
42 Markham Place
London W3
(044-1) 234-8730

Internet 35466.5202 @ COMPUSERVE.COM

WORK EXPERIENCE

1994 - Present	CHASE INVESTMENT BANK: London, U.K. Managing Director

Arranged a $500 million multiple option facility for the Kingdom of Spain. Originated ten Eurobond issues throughout the EEC for U.S. and European multinationals. Arranged and syndicated a ten-year S.F. $100 million loan swap transaction.

1986 - 1994	THE CHASE MANHATTAN BANK, N.A.: New York, NY
1991 - 1994	Vice President - Swiss Institutional Banking

Managed eleven person team overseeing employer's relationship with 150 Swiss and Lichtenstein banks. Negotiated over $100 million in new documentary business. Coordinated five-year European Strategic Plan. Honored by Consortium of Swiss Bankers for effective planning.

1989 - 1991	Vice President - International Trade Finance

Created and implemented innovative approach to extending credit in conjunction with the World Bank. Developed new financial risk participation product to increase trade finance business. Coordinated employer's worldwide financial activities with World Bank and IMF.

1986 - 1989	Second Vice President - Corporate Foreign Direct

Managed employer's relationship with U.S. subsidiaries of French and Swiss multinationals. Developed $30 million portfolio of high quality financial assets. Directed marketing that resulted in 20% increase in free business.

EDUCATION

1986	New York University: New York, NY M.B.A.
1982	Williams College: Williamstown, MA B.A.

LANGUAGES

Fluent in French - read, speak, and write.

GORDON A. LIPPOLIS
55 Beuer Court
Cambridge, MA 02140
(617) 555-9097
(617) 555-6000, ext. 46; fax - 555-6332

EXPERIENCE

1984 - Present   ARNOLD BURNHAM & COMPANY: Boston, MA

Senior Analyst

- Conducted statistical analyses affecting investment programs of public, industrial, and financial institutions.
- Interpreted data concerning investment prices, yields, stability, and future trends using daily stock and bond reports.
- Researched and analyzed losses and adverse financial trends, using AOL and the Internet.
- Devised "value line" for utility stocks based on relationship of dividends to bond interest rates.
- Acted as chief analyst in textile industry.

1972 - 1984   GEMSTONE SILK, INC.: New York, NY

Chief Executive

- Responsible for firm-wide sales of $10 million, including textile weaving, converting, and marketing.
- Developed processing innovations resulting in substantial cost reductions.
- As Vice President, set up data processing system for inventory and production control and sales analysis.
- Also held positions of Vice President, Plant Manager, and Technician.
- As Plant Manager, initiated new testing program for laboratory standards.
- As Technician, developed new materials for use in Navy aircraft.

EDUCATION/TRAINING

1987   M.I.T.
Investment Analysis

1986   New York Institute of Finance
Portfolio Management

1982   New York University
Linear Programming

ELLIOT R. MADISON
1222 Hickory Drive
Seville, CO 81009
(303) 555-5424 - phone & fax

JOB TARGET   REHABILITATIVE PHYSIOTHERAPIST

CAPABILITIES

- Determine appropriate treatment for muscular injuries.
- Accurately diagnose sprains, strains, and ruptures.
- Prepare detailed home-care programs.
- Train loss-of-limb patients in use and care of prosthetic devices.
- Instill motivation in newly handicapped patients.
- Train medical personnel in basics of physical therapy.
- Accurately evaluate physician's recommendations.
- Administer therapy by light, heat, water, and electricity.
- Effectively use ultrasound and diathermy equipment.

ACCOMPLISHMENTS

- Diagnosed and successfully treated hundreds of patients.
- Performed extensive patient tests and evaluations such as range of motion, functional analyses, and body parts measurements.
- Administered a variety of massage techniques, deep and superficial.
- Administered traction equipment to patients.
- Prepared accurate records of patient treatment and progress.
- Fitted patients with orthotics.
- Trained patients in manual therapeutic exercises for home care.
- Assisted patients in adjusting daily activities to support their condition.

WORK HISTORY

1990 - Present   ST. MARY'S HOSPITAL: Seville, CO
Colorado Staff Physical Therapist

1990   UNIVERSITY OF MICHIGAN MEDICAL CENTER: Ann Arbor, MI
Intern Physical Therapist

EDUCATION

1990   UNIVERSITY OF MICHIGAN
B.S. - Physical Therapy

1990   Certificate of Physical Therapy

REBECCA HOWELL

34465 Avennal Way
Washington, DC 20034
(202) 555-5411 - Phone and Fax

JOB TARGET   Program Development for Mental Health Field

CAPABILITIES

- Design and develop training materials.
- Develop LPN level remedial training tactics.
- Write clear and concise proposals for grant monies.
- Administer and evaluate various cognitive skills tests.
- Consult with psychologists and clients.
- Counsel teenagers, troubled and disadvantaged youth.
- Design and deliver oral presentation to large groups.

ACHIEVEMENTS

- Designed and wrote training manual for the care of isolated patients in nursing homes.
- Created awareness training program for airline personnel to foster better understanding of handicapped passengers' needs.
- Wrote proposal for the training of counselors working with ex-offenders, resulting in $250M federal funding.
- Administered and evaluated tests including the Wexler and MMPI, to ex-offenders and high school students.
- Developed psychological and skills profiles consulting with psychologists on test results and broad spectrum interpretations.
- Referred clients successfully to various self-help organizations as a result of testing.
- Counseled 50 teenagers in pregnancy prevention and prenatal care.
- Delivered lectures to various community organizations on the need to support mental health programs.

WORK HISTORY

1993 - Present   Health Organizations
Volunteer in community and mental health groups

1991 - 1993   PIEDMONT AIRLINES
Consultant in Awareness Training for Handicapped

EDUCATION

GEORGE WASHINGTON UNIVERSITY
M.S. - Social Services

MARSHALL ULLMAN
341 Genesee Street
Rochester, NY 14610
(716) 555-7753; AOL MARSHUMAN

JOB TARGET   Personal Trainer / Body-Builder for Health Clubs

CAPABILITIES

- Diagnose new and existing member health and fitness problems; prescribe comprehensive programs for meeting client needs.
- Set long-term goals for clients, promoting extended memberships.
- Increase club members' commitment and deliver multiple referrals.
- Design beginner, intermediate, and advanced personal fitness programs with the added knowlege of medical disciplines.
- Instruct in the proper use of exercise equipment while demonstrating correct form and technique.
- Develop individualized manual therapeutic exercise programs.

ACCOMPLISHMENTS

- Personal fitness trainer consulting 150 clients for more than three years.
- Diagnosed and treated sports-related injuries.
- Established and presented Sports Injury Awareness workshops in five high school athletic programs. Injuries decreased 50% in first year.
- Won the Junior Mr. Atlantic U.S.A. Body-Building Championship, in 1989.
- Lectured for the Upstate Sports Massage Team, Rochester School of Ballet, and Onondaga County Community College.

WORK HISTORY

1995 - Present	Personal Training Consultant Rochester, NY
1991 - Present	Chiropractor - Private Practice Rochester, NY
1989 - 1991	Health Education Instructor Syracuse City School System: Syracuse, NY

EDUCATION

1991	Los Angeles Chiropractic College Doctorate
1989	Syracuse University B.S. - Health Education

CHERYL WOOLSEY
14 Rosewood Lane
Garden City, NY 11530
(516) 555-7280 - phone & fax

JOB TARGET   HOSPITAL ADMINISTRATOR

CAPABILITIES

- Handle in-depth coordinating and planning.
- Direct complex activities in operations and finance.
- Operate successfully with hospitals, managed care facilities, HIP, Fortune 500 industrial, and commercial operations.
- Manage commercial medical administration for headquarters as well as divisions.
- Act as liaison among diverse groups.
- Establish and maintain excellent budget reports.

ACCOMPLISHMENTS

- Developed and implemented policies and procedures for eight medical centers serving 125,000 HIP subscribers.
- Recruited and hired administrative staff for eight centers.
- Assisted Chief Administrator in training program preparation.
- Prepared and maintained capital project status and budget reports for New York City's 18 hospitals and care centers.
- Communicated directly with Executive Directors.
- Acted as liaison officer with contractors, vendors, and department heads, interrelating with medical staff regarding their needs.
- Coordinated multi-shop activities for a major health care complex.
- Established an on-site office for a major missile producer.
- Recruited, trained, and directed employees responsible for stocking missile site with capital equipment spare parts.

WORK EXPERIENCE

1990 - Present	PAN BOROUGH HOSPITAL CENTER Maintenance Control Planner	New York, NY
1983 - 1990	LA JUANIA MEDICAL GROUP Administrative Coordinator	New York, NY
1981 - 1983	NEW YORK CITY HOSPITALS CORP. Planning Analyst	New York, NY

EDUCATION

C.C.N.Y. - Liberal Arts

RUFUS JACKSON
11 Holly Hock Road
South Bend, Indiana 46637
(317) 555-4562 home (317) 555-7000 office

PROFESSIONAL EXPERIENCE

1990 - Present   Warehouse Coordinator
NOTRE DAME UNIVERSITY: South Bend, Indiana
Responsible for surplus equipment for the University and
three hospitals associated with the ND Medical Center, with
equipment inventory of $800,000. Coordinate "open and
closed bid" sales and auctions on a regular basis to liquidate
inventory. Proceeds amount to $350,000 annually.

1990 - Present   Fleet Manager and Warehouse Supervisor
FORT BENJAMIN HARRISON: South Bend, Indiana
Forwarded military support elements for the Special Olympic
Games. Researched prices, contacted vendors, and made
vendor recommendations concerning equipment
procurement. Coordinated delivery and pickup of equipment
between civilian and military personnel. Designed blueprints
and specifications for a 15,000 s.f. warehouse and an 8500 s.f.
kennel. Scheduled daily use of 76 military vehicles and
scheduled required maintenance. Monitored vehicle mileage
and use to assure project budget did not exceed $500,000.
Supervised 20 people daily.

1986 - 1990   Maintenance/Supply Coordinator
UNITED STATES ARMY: Philippines and WV bases
Provided technical assistance concerning aircraft parts.
Researched manuals and other sources to locate suitable
replacement parts and materials. Served as liaison between
maintenance and supply personnel. Supervised 10-15 aircraft
mechanics and supply personnel daily.

1975 - 1986   Maintenance/Material Control Supervisor
UNITED STATES ARMY: WV and Worldwide Army bases
Advised and counseled high school students on career
opportunities in the United States Army. Directed scheduled
and unscheduled maintenance for 24 aircraft. Provided
support to pilots concerning aircraft readiness. Authorized
aircraft's safety for flight. Supervised eight people daily.

EDUCATION

1992   NOTRE DAME UNIVERSITY: South Bend, IN
Bachelor - General Studies
Major: Government Procurement; GPA 3.32

MICHAEL THOMAS
468 Pelham Road
New Rochelle, NY 10805
(914) 555-5313 COMPUSERVE 41125,8906

1987 - Present	**WESTCHESTER COUNTY PAROLE BOARD** Pelham, NY

Narcotics Parole Officer

Engaged in the rehabilitation of an average caseload of 40 certified addicts. Developed individualized programs for each client, according to need. This involved one-on-one counseling as well as frequent contact with client's family, incorporating them into treatment plan.

Created jobs for clients through contact with community agencies such as Operation Upgrade and Cellblock Theatre. Provided training in basic job skills as Operation Comeback and Office of Vocational Rehabilitation.

1981 - 1987	**WESTCHESTER COUNTY SOCIAL SERVICES** Rye, NY

Casework Supervisor/Caseworker

Supervised fifteen caseworkers in Emergency Services caseload. Trained them in agency procedures and casework techniques. Responsible for managing 300 active cases in the unit. Maintained controls for numerous required reports. Created time management system for employees to organize their work for maximum productivity.

Provided needed services as a caseworker for families seeking public assistance. Counseled clients individually, gearing the goal to fit each need. Set up special services such as employment, basic education, and nursing homes. Maintained accurate and complete records on each client.

Achieved highest record in casework unit in one year for clients' removal from public assistance roles.

EDUCATION

1981	ST. JOHN'S UNIVERSITY: Long Island, NY B.B.A.
AWARDS	Patrolmen's Benevolent Association Good Samaritan

CLAUDE LOGUE
2240 Rhodes Avenue
St. Louis, MO 63109
(314) 555-2155

ORGANIZATION
Initiated a supervised education placement in court advocacy; organized recruitment and training of volunteers; coordinated liaison between court officials, social agency, and media. Chaired a student committee on social concerns and arranged special lecture series. Programmed and evaluated a video-taped panel discussion for student leaders and university administrators.

COMMUNICATION
Presented to city officials a statement urging approval of overnight shelter facility. Described court experience of assault victims in local TV appearance; wrote newsletter article on function of court volunteers. Designed and directed worship services for hospital patients. Assisted in preparing article series on graduate student living.

COUNSELING
Provided staff support for director of family shelter. Assisted hospital personnel in dealing with illness and death. Aided abuse victims in sharing their experience. Guided homeless families toward personal and community resources. Related to students' concerns for healthy lifestyle and meaningful vocation.

EXPERIENCE
1993 - 1996   Administrative Assistant
                Overnight Shelter: St. Louis, MO

1990   Research Interviewer
                Project on Homelessness: St. Louis, MO

1990   Program Assistant
                Education Department, American Red Cross: St. Louis, MO

1989 - 1990   Assistant Director
                Family Shelter: Fayetteville, NC

1989   Chaplain Intern
                Kain Medical Center: Fayetteville, NC

EDUCATION
- M.Div. Theology/Philosophy, Union Theological Seminary, St. Louis, MO
- B.S., Botany/Art History, University of North Carolina, Fayetteville, NC
- Specialized training in the development of programs educating clergy on topic of family violence, Atlanta, GA

JENNIFER ALLEN
2260 Rominia Avenue
St. Louis, Missouri 63109
(314) 555-7602

COUNSELING

- Coordinated corporate outplacement center.
- Assisted clients in conducting career evaluation while performing directive counseling.
- Developed clients' resumes and implemented successful self-marketing strategies, resulting in 30 day placements.
- Identified and researched potential employers and specific corporate hiring authorities.
- Provided psychological support for recently terminated employees.

ADMINISTRATIVE MANAGEMENT

- Supervised office activities while ensuring efficient operation of small publishing and sales promotion company.
- Coordinated sales and management seminars throughout the U.S., including travel and facilities arrangements.
- Developed and maintained customer relations.
- Coordinated production and sales of books and other promotional and educational materials.

PUBLIC RELATIONS/COMMUNITY SERVICE

- Assisted coordinator of special services for a national health organization.
- Promoted events and conducted public relations and fund-raising for a nationally recognized regional theater company.
- Coordinated volunteer activities, including recruitment, for a private hospital's major fund-raiser. Raised in excess of $150,000 annually.

WORK HISTORY

1982 - present   Professional Volunteer
MO Job Center; and Children's Hospital: St. Louis, MO

1982 - present   Volunteer Fund-Raiser
Repertory Theater of St. Louis: Webster Groves, MO

Previous   Assistant Copywriter, Leviathan Newsletter
UNIVERSITY OF ILLINOIS: Urbana, IL

EDUCATION

1974   UNIVERSITY OF ILLINOIS: Urbana, IL
B.A. - Journalism with Advertising Emphasis

JAMES C. CURRY
670 Marantha Way
Allentown, PA 18106
(215) 555- 3349; AOL JAMCUR

NON-PROFIT ADMINISTRATION
- Over twenty-five years of management and administrative experience.
- Vice-president and committee chair for three nonprofit organizations.
- Coordinated and delegated over two hundred volunteers for three nonprofit organizations.
- Certified in nonprofit administration.

COMMUNICATION
- Made group presentations to gain approval and funding for three nonprofit organizations.
- Wrote grant proposal, evaluated direct mail campaign, wrote news releases for the Allentown Public Library.
- Compiled and edited production, budget, and customer satisfaction reports for catalog division of retail store.
- Served as liaison between bookstore, staff, faculty, and college directors.

MANAGEMENT
- Coordinated and delegated over two hundred volunteers for three nonprofit organizations.
- Managed three bookstores, purchased stock, trained and supervised twelve employees; responsible for $400,000 volume.
- Managed and operated successful paint contracting business, prepared cost projections, payroll and business reports.
- Supervised, trained, and evaluated ten employees, maintained inventory and production quotas for catalog division of retail store.

WORK HISTORY
1988 - present   Bookbuyer
                               Moffet College Books

1984 - 1994   Painting Contractor
                               Self-Employed

                               Non-profit history: Intern - Allentown Public Library
                               Vice-President / Committee Chairman - St. Mark's Lutheran Church
                               Committee Chairman - Boy Scouts
                               Speaker Bureau Volunteer - Alleco Action Center

EDUCATION/PROFESSIONAL DEVELOPMENT
1986   Muhlenberg College
                               Certificate - Nonprofit Administration

                               Penn State University
                               B.A.; Member - Pennsylvania Association of Non-Profit Organizations (PENPO)

SUSAN CRANSTON DOUGLASS

345-47 Melbourne Street
Jackson Heights, NY 11328
212-555-5120 - phone & fax

LIBRARY CONSULTING

Revised and edited author catalog. Verified entries in bibliographic sources. Set up outreach program that resulted in 30% greater use of library. Conducted senior citizens seminars that included extensive use of audiovisual materials. Handled book selection and ordering. Processed gift books and film programming. Developed and administered high school English language library.

LIBRARY RESEARCH & REFERENCE

Handled extensive reference work in social and behavioral sciences. Trained numerous small groups in use of reference sources such as card or book catalogue or book and periodical indexes to locate information. Demonstrated procedures for searching catalog files. Serviced government documents. Maintained vertical and curriculum files as well as film programs and book reviewing.

WORK HISTORY

1995 - 1996   AMERICAN MUSEUM OF ANCIENT HISTORY LIBRARY
Consultant

1990 - 1995   QUEENSBOROUGH PUBLIC LIBRARY
Library Consultant

PUBLICATIONS

- *Author Catalogue;* Jewish Museum of History for their library.
- *Americans and Their History*: American Library Association.

EDUCATION

1992   QUEENS COLLEGE
Masters - Library Science

1989   B.A. - History

JANE SIMPKINS
335 Warren Avenue
Spring Lake, NJ 07762
(201) 555-5881 Compuserve 96675, 6798

COUNSELING

- Consulted with parents for probable child abuse and suggested courses of action.
- Partnered with social workers on individual cases in both urban and suburban settings.
- Counseled single parents on appropriate coping behavior.
- Handled pre-intake interviewing of many individual abused children.

TEACHING

- Instructed large and diverse community groups on issues related to child abuse.
- Taught 30 volunteers to set up community child abuse programs.
- Ran workshops for parents of abused children.
- Instructed public school teachers on signs and symptoms of potential child abuse.

ORGANIZATION/COORDINATION

- Coordinated transition of children between original and foster homes.
- Served as liaison and child abuse educator between community health agencies and schools.
- Wrote proposal to state for county funds to educate single parents and teachers. Funding accepted.

VOLUNTEER WORK HISTORY

1990 - 1996   Volunteer Coordinator - Child Abuse Program
COMMUNITY MENTAL HEALTH CENTER
Freehold, NJ

1989 - 1990   County Representative
C.A.R.E. - Child-Abuse-Rescue-Education
Albany Park, NJ

EDUCATION

1981   Douglass College: New Brunswick, NJ
B.S. - Sociology

TERI R. GAVINDER
55 Northgate Street
Atlanta, GA 30341
(404) 555-4522

JOB TARGET   COMMUNITY RELATIONS DIRECTOR

CAPABILITIES

- Promote public understanding and support for programs and services.
- Organize and direct fund-raising campaigns.
- Write press releases, informational brochures, and other public relations materials.
- Give presentations, speeches, and workshops to public, private, and nonprofit organizations.
- Establish contacts with local print, radio, and TV news editors.
- Recruit and train volunteer workers.
- Prepare budgets, administer projects, and review results with Project 4.0.

ACCOMPLISHMENTS

- Built a personal contact network including CEOs and executive directors of over 50 local private businesses and community-service organizations.
- Coordinated the United Way Volunteers' fund-raising campaign that raised over $250,000 for health, education, and AIDS awareness programs.
- Recruited 2,000+ volunteers over the last six years to work in a variety of school-related programs.
- Won Distinguished Community Service Award from the Atlanta Cultural Affairs Commission.

EXPERIENCE

1992 - present   UNITED WAY OF ATLANTA: Atlanta, GA
Community Services Volunteer

1988 - 1994   ATLANTA METROPOLITAN SCHOOLS: Atlanta, GA
Chair-Volunteer Programs

EDUCATION

1981   EMORY UNIVERSITY: Atlanta, GA
B.A. - English

CAROLE SMYTHE HANOVER

1332 Linden Place North
Chicago, IL 60647
(312) 555-8978

TEACHING EXPERIENCE

1990 - Present   ST. SEBASTIAN SCHOOL: Chicago, IL

- Design lessons and instruct in all subjects appropriate for grade level. Adapt and create learning materials to meet the needs of diverse student competencies. Organize Career Week for fifth grade class, recruiting community workers as speakers. Plan and accompany students on field trips.

- Provide interesting activities for special holidays and ethnic celebrations as approved by the board curriculum. Science includes timely information, such as communicable disease awareness and prevention.

- Write illustrated class newsletter for open and frequent communication with parents. Maintain attractive classroom, meaningful bulletin boards, and special learning areas.

- Received "superior" rating in management, leadership and creativity from school principal.

1989 - 1990   CHICAGO BOARD OF EDUCATION

- Substitute Teacher. Implemented lesson plans as provided by permanent teacher to promote continuity.

CHICAGOLAND MARITIME MUSEUM

- Instructor and Tour Guide. Gave historical and scientific presentations to all age groups. Trained 20 Instructors.

VOLUNTEER ACTIVITIES
Sunday School Teacher, St. Timothy's (1 year) Lutheran Bible School (2 summers)

PROFESSIONAL GROWTH
Participated in Workshops in Language Arts Methods, Creative Writing, Ethics, Learning Disabilities, Classroom Management

CERTIFICATIONS
Chicago Board of Education, Elementary
Illinois State Board, K-9, Type 3
Archdiocese of Chicago, Elementary

EDUCATION
University of Illinois: Urbana, IL
B.S. Elementary Education - Early Childhood Education

JILL GOLDMAN
2156 42nd Street
Brooklyn, NY 11218
(718) 555-3214 - messages

JOB TARGET   READING CONSULTANT - ELEMENTARY SCHOOL

CAPABILITIES

- Prepare outlines for daily and monthly course of study.
- Lecture and demonstrate with audiovisual teaching aids.
- Prepare, administer, and correct reading tests.
- Maintain order and discipline in large and small classes.
- Counsel and direct children with reading difficulties.
- Counsel parents and direct them into remedial action for specific cognitive or emotional problems of children.
- Train and develop children in verbal self-expression.

ACHIEVEMENTS

- Cited as Teacher of the Year in 1991 in a school of 800 students.
- Trained two learning-disabled children to achieve full integration in public school class within two months.
- Tutored six "underachievers" in remedial reading; all six finished in upper 30% of class by end of year.
- Developed new system for reporting reading comprehension analyses now used in school system city-wide.
- Introduced audiovisual techniques for math learning into Grade 2 with great success.

WORK HISTORY

1988 - Present   YESHIVA HAVRAM SECULAR DIVISION: Brooklyn, NY
Fifth and Sixth Grade Teacher

1987   DOWD COMMUNICATIONS: New York, NY
Production Assistant

EDUCATION

1987   New York University
M.S. - Education - Emphasis on Elementary Ed Reading
B.A. - Sociology - Minor in Elementary Education

JOSEPHINE CARAWAY
87309 Castleberry Place
Affton, MO 63123
(314) 555-2154

Work History

1987 - Present   HOLY REDEEMER LUTHERAN CHURCH: Affton, MO
Church began as a mission congregation and has grown to over 350 members.

Pastoral Assistant, Confirmation Teacher

Served in all administrative and specific education functions. Activities included office administration, coordination duties, secretarial support and church council.

1981 - Present   PUBLIC SCHOOL TEACHING

1994 - Present	Substitute Teacher
1983 - 1987	Third and Fourth Grades
1982 - 1983	Teacher's Aide
1981 - 1982	Third and Fourth Grades

Pastoral Administration and Education

- Serve as Sunday School Superintendent. Oversee all education and supervisory needs of a very successful program that includes over 100 primary-grade children.
- Served as chairperson after developing the Christian Education Committee that is responsible for all Christian education from three-year-olds to adults.
- Regularly taught Sunday School and Confirmation classes ranging in size from 10 to 20 students.
- Developed and directed Vacation Bible School. Specifically worked with a team of six teachers to write and choose curriculum. Coordinated student registration, ordered materials and collected tuition.

Formal Education

Continuing graduate work at the University of Missouri.

University of Missouri
B.S. with High Honors - Elementary Education

Admitted to Phi Beta Kappa Society.
Studied abroad at Redland College, Bristol, England.

Studied "On the Write Road" and "Discipline with Love and Logic" through Webster University

DEBRA G. HARNER
211 East Haley Street
Philadelphia, PA 19146
(215) 555-9990 office; (215) 555-9998 fax
(215) 555-6784 home & fax

1990 - Present   **Executive Vice President**, Programs for Employers
                   IMPETUS, INC.: Philadelphia, PA

Managed all administrative operations. Directed the work of five functional
units, 750 employees. Active in formulation and implementation of
organizational policy. Planned, developed, and evaluated programs.
Developed and designed programs and materials. Prepared brochures and
other promotional material to increase sales. Used teleconferencing software
to increase statistical outputs 120%.

1983 - 1990   **Corporate Director of Operations**
                   NATIONAL RESEARCH & DEVELOPMENT
                   CORPORATION: Philadelphia, PA

Managed all educational and manpower projects. Assisted project directors in
all technical management functions. Prepared proposals for both private and
public funding up to $20MM. Negotiated contracts. Evaluated on-site
operations to ensure effective implementation of contractual requirements.

1982 - 1983   **Director of Research**, Office of Inspection
                   OFFICE OF ECONOMICS - CITY OF NEW YORK

Organized and maintained an early warning system to identify local
community action problems for agency director. Coordinated national
inspection visits. Prepared research reports for the agency's congressional
presentation.

EDUCATION
            MIAMI UNIVERSITY: Oxford, OH
            B.A. - Honors in English

MEMBERSHIPS
            National Association of Research & Development
            Professionals

SARAH O'ROURKE
Rt 3, Box 234
Princeton, WV 24740
(304) 555-5542 (304) 555-8875 FAX

SALES & MARKETING
- Assisted in the planning and implementation of several Open House Weekends for 150-250 prospective college students.
- Conducted campus tours and interviews with prospective students and their families.
- Planned and implemented a dealership service clinic for 45 current and prospective customers.
- Prepared a marketing cost-effectiveness study for a college Admissions Office.
- Sold cameras and video equipment on a retail level and averaged in the top third among the sales staff.

RECORD-KEEPING
- Maintained the accounting records and prepared monthly financial statements for a company with five separate profit centers and average annual gross sales of $19,000,000.
- Prepared payroll and maintained records for 75 employees.
- Prepared monthly and quarterly financial statements for five different companies.
- Reconciled daily cash reports for a hotel and restaurant with average daily sales of $8,000.

SUPERVISION
- Supervised a staff of 38 waiters and waitresses for large banquets.
- Trained, scheduled and supervised a staff of up to 30 campus tour guides.
- Managed a business office staff of four bookkeepers and computer operators.

WORK HISTORY
1988 - Present   BOOKKEEPER / CONTROLLER
R.K. Denver & Co.: Princeton, WV

1985 - 1988   SALES MANAGER
Cassidy Photo: Tallahassee, FL

EDUCATION   Davis & Elkins College: Elkins, WV
B.A. - Accounting/Finance

JENNIFER MARSHALL
23-13 114th Street
Richmond Hill, NY 11418
(718) 555-4461

JOB TARGET
Administrative Coordinator - Fashion Design Merchandising

MARKETING/MERCHANDISING
- Provided merchandising and marketing support to 400 sales reps.
- Compiled and reviewed sales data.
- Made marketing recommendations to employer.
- Developed new product demonstrations using graphics software.
- Created merchandising and showroom design.
- Sketched design concepts for upcoming product lines.

ADMINISTRATION
- Screen publication materials for editorial review.
- Make recommendations for publication from submittals.
- Review and determine legitimacy of contest applications.
- Ensure accuracy of computer system for purchase orders.

ORGANIZATION
- Effectively process and direct telephone communications for staff of 125.
- Coordinate and implement mailings and special projects.
- Organized conferences and seminars for national cosmetic firm.

COMMUNICATIONS
- Acted as liaison between design, production and shipping departments.
- Train reception personnel.
- Welcome visitors; respond to and direct public inquiries.
- Perform initial screening of job applicants.
- Administer and grade employee aptitude tests.

EMPLOYMENT HISTORY
1995 - Present   CONDE-NAST, INC.: New York, NY
                  Receptionist

1993 - 1995   YOUTHSPRINGS SPORTSWEAR: New York, NY
                  Production Coordinator

1988 - 1990   LINDA LIGHT COSMETICS: Philadelphia, PA
                  Marketing Assistant

EDUCATION
1993   BARD COLLEGE: Annandale, NY
                  B.A. - Merchandising

HEATHER MANGANARO
1563 Lindell Boulevard
St. Louis, MO 63110
phone (314) 555-2639; fax (314) 555-2676

WORK HISTORY

1992 - Present   WASHINGTON UNIVERSITY
School of Continuing Education: St. Louis, MO

Director of Program Development

Designed and staffed 40 programs focused on business and career development. Redesigned the career program to include: personnel management, basic and advanced career workshops, arts management, communication skills for secretaries, fund raising and grantsmanship.

Managerial and administrative responsibilities include: course conceptualization and design, faculty hiring and salary negotiation, administrative staff supervision, public relations, location selection, and space negotiation.

1990 - 1992   WNAL-FM RADIO STATION: Clayton, MO

Program Producer/Host

Originated VOICES, a weekly radio show focused on human development and public affairs. Topics include: career and life planning, women and management, EEO, Title IX, book and film discussion and reviews, job satisfaction, adult life stages, and the quality of work life.

Production and administrative responsibilities included: research of topics, development of discussion formats, selection and scheduling of guests, promotion on air and off, and interviewing.

1986 - 1990   CLAYTON CENTRAL SCHOOL DISTRICT: Clayton, MO

Humanities Instructor

Improved student performance and teacher accountability. Developed and implemented innovative learning contracts incorporating needs assessment, performance objectives, and joint student/teacher evaluation procedures.

EDUCATION

1986   St. Louis University
B.A. - M.A. in progress

DIANNE L. BISHOP
221 North Lake Avenue
Detroit, MI 48221
(313) 555-6774 FAX-(313) 555-6773

JOB TARGET   Director of Development

CAPABILITIES
- Direct capital campaigns, feasibility studies, annual giving drives, and planned-giving programs.
- Write speeches, case statement brochures, and giant proposals.
- Conduct interviews, tabulate and analyze findings, write reports, and present conclusions and recommendations.
- Teach, advise, and counsel students on academic and personal concerns.

ACCOMPLISHMENTS
- Organized and conducted a capital campaign to raise $600,000 in individual contributions for a private school in Detroit, MI; completed the campaign in less than four months and exceeded goals by 25%.
- Set up and implemented a planned-giving program in conjunction with a $4 million capital campaign for a not-for-profit hospital.
- Planned long-range development program to raise $300,000 (20% of operating expenses) for nonprofit arts organization. Wrote grants to secure additional $125,000 from county, state, and federal sources.
- Advised clients on integrating annual campaigns with capital campaigns as well as programs for securing special grants, major gifts, and planned or deferred gifts.

WORK HISTORY
1993 - present   WARNER & ASSOCIATES: Detroit, MI
Consulting Associate

1984 - 1993   WENTWORTH ACADEMY: Detroit, MI
Director of Development

1977 - 1984   WENTWORTH ACADEMY: Detroit, MI
Assistant Development Director

EDUCATION
1976   PRINCETON UNIVERSITY: Princeton, NJ
M.B.A.

RENEE DAVIS MONTANA
355 Kennedy Avenue
Boston, MA 02148
(617) 555-5331 FAX (617) 555-5131

JOB TARGET   Director of International Sales

CAPABILITIES

- Utilize extensive knowledge of the specialty Cheese/Supermarket Deli industry in the U. S. and Europe.
- Establish major accounts and manage regional brokers.
- Analyze sales statistics to develop specific objectives for accounts.
- Plan and formulate pricing programs to increase gross profitability.
- Develop and implement marketing strategies and design promotional programs.
- Train broker sales representatives and conduct seminars for supermarket account personnel.
- Fluent in French and Spanish.

ACCOMPLISHMENTS

- Established and maintained accounts with over 35 major customers encompassing all major supermarket chains in New England and Upstate New York.
- Increased annual sales from $1.1 million to $5.5 million in four years.
- Planned and coordinated approximately $750K in co-op advertising funds annually.
- Planned and conducted "Cheese School" seminars at key accounts.
- Managed Cheese Department in a specialty gourmet shop for five years; developed extensive knowledge in product handling, merchandising, and customer relations.

WORK HISTORY

1994 - present   GORDON-ROSS FOODS, INC: Boston, MA
                   New England Sales Manager

1990 - 1994   ROSS FOODS, INC: Boston, MA
                   Telemarketer/Telemarketing Supervisor

1985 - 1990   THE WINERY: Santa Fe, NM
                   Assistant Store Manager

EDUCATION

1985   SALEM STATE COLLEGE: Salem, MA
                   Marketing Management

DONALD LOGGINS
22 Old Hickory Lane
Princeton, NJ 08504
(609) 555-5562 FAX (609) 555-5353

WORK HISTORY

1980 - Present	**ADAMSBORO INDUSTRIES**: Princeton, NJ
1987 - Present	Vice President, Marketing Services

Instituted change in Consumer Division pricing policies resulting in company reaffirmation as industry leader. Sales $8.2M. Established effective communication strategy among all corporate departments eliminating redundancy, and increasing organizational effectiveness. Initiated distribution methods study saving $845K and improving customer services. Coordinated facilities relocation and incorporated automated and computer-assisted materials handling system, saving company $3.1M. Implemented computerized electronic system allowing accounts to order directly via on-site terminals. Restructured company graphics division reducing expenses by $410K. Redirected educational department emphasis to serve wider populations involving direct accounts as well as institutions.

1980 - 1987	Sales Controller

Realigned company into appropriate divisions; analyzed allocated expenses into P and L responsibility.

1974 - 1980	**GENERAL SYSTEMS CORPORATION**: New York, NY

Controller - International Division

Established accounting system for 62 foreign franchises.

PROFESSIONAL AFFILIATIONS

American Management Club, Sales Executive Club (SEC)

EDUCATION

Hofstra University
B.B.A. - Business Administration

Professional seminars/training in: sales, management, retail, computer technology

MICHELLE BRAILSFORD
533 Walser Road
Louisville, KY 40207
(502) 555-6700, EXT 21; FAX (502) 555-6740

EXPERIENCE

1994 - Present   SALES REPRESENTATIVE
                       The Silverton Company: Louisville, KY
Establish print advertising in account locations to generate consumer trail and usage.
Prepare and deliver presentations to increase sales, distribution, and consumer impact.
Independently manage personal field office. Accountabilities include time management
and efficiently coordinating administrative services from local vendors. Serve as one point
of contact to all Silverton grocers, wholesalers, and end users for over 100 products in
each account. Awarded Salesperson of the Quarter, from 27 salespeople, after first full
quarter with company. Won national second prize in Fall 1995 Creative Display Contest.

1993 - 1994   SALES SERVICE COORDINATOR
                       Electro-Globe: Louisville, KY
Attended training program hosted by two shut-down facilities of corporate consolidation.
Managed eight large O.E.M. sales accounts. Dramatically reduced customer billing claims
through innovative group process intervention. Answered 50-100 calls per day interfacing
with customers, sales, marketing, and manufacturing.

1992 - 1993   INTERN
                       Kentucky Power and Light Company: Lexington, KY
Received one of two internship programs offered. Administered and facilitated stand-up
classroom training. Developed permanent course material on motivation for Fundamentals
of Effective Supervision course. Developed and statistically analyzed course evaluations
for Total Quality and Management Development classes. Developed draft of company's
first-ever comprehensive training needs analysis to assess needs of over 8,000 employees.

1991 - 1993   SALES ASSOCIATE
                       The Railroad Shop: Lexington, KY
Worked at second job while attending college. Consistently led sales force in sale dollars
per purchase, sales per hour, and items per purchase.

EDUCATION

June 1993   University of Kentucky: Lexington, KY
                       B.A. - Human Resource Development
                       G.P.A. in major 3.6/4.0

CIVIC/PROFESSIONAL

- American Management Association, member
- American Society for Training and Development, national and local member
- National Association for Female Executives, professional member
- Literacy Volunteers of America, certified active tutor
- Center for the Study of the Presidency member. Invited to attend 1993 conference "The U.S. and the Pacific Rim."

SUSAN SOLLOWAY
321 Fort Washington Avenue
New York, NY 10033
(212) 555-7743 AOL SOLLO2

WORK EXPERIENCE

1987 - Present	LEISURE TRAVEL SALES, INC: New York, NY

Sales/Marketing:

Develop wholesale travel department. Focus on individual and group travel programs for executives, employees, groups, civic and fraternal organizations. Design incentive programs for sales force within companies.

Advertising:

Evaluate profitability of advertising strategy. Responsible for selecting best vehicles for copy and promotion. Utilize demographical information and readership data of trade publications and journals for determining advertising campaign. Personally write ad copy for major ad projects.

Research:

Examine which specific facilities and destinations would best service each group's style, budget, and conference needs. Survey industries, and develop individual presentations for conference planning.

Budgeting:

Plan budgets for each program. Negotiate hotel contracts. Cost out internal operational expenses (reservations, documentation, ticketing, itinerary planning). Budget out advertising expenditures from copywriting to final printing and placement stages. Reduced operational costs by 20% in first year of program.

1983 - 1987	BIGGER MAN APPAREL, INC.: Orange, CT

Customer Service Representative

Responsible for all manufacturing sources meeting delivery deadline obligations. Functions included merchandising, pricing, buying, and general sales. Worked on all phases of company advertising.

EDUCATION

1983	ADELPHI UNIVERSITY: Garden City, NY B.A. - Liberal Arts

JOELLEN MARKOWSKI
57 Waverly Court
San Francisco, CA 94507
(415) 555-8900 (messages)

SALES/RETAIL

- Developed promotional campaigns for new product lines.
- Increased sales by $500,000 in nine-month period.
- Coordinated accounts of over 20 large department stores.
- Sold specialty clothing for West Coast shop dealing with special, hard-to-fit clients.

MANAGEMENT

- Organized and implemented a program for 40 college students abroad.
- Coordinated student/faculty liaison relationship.
- Managed an inventory of several thousand items.
- Trained and supervised three assistants.

WRITING

- Wrote several free-lance articles for a California daily.
- Composed correspondence in French as well as in English.
- Fluent in reading, writing, and speaking French, Spanish, and Italian.

EXPERIENCE

1991 - Present   COQ AU VIN GOURMET CLUB: Tiburon, CA
Promotional Sales

1990   LA PANACHE BOUTIQUE: San Francisco, CA
Salesperson

EDUCATION

1991   UNIVERSITY OF CALIFORNIA AT BERKELEY
B.A. - Liberal Arts

MARK ATWOOD SHERMAN, C.F.A.
78 Rutgers Drive
Port Washington, NY 11050
(516) 555-4461
COMPUSERVE MARKMAN @AOL.COM

EXPERIENCE

1990 - Present

W.B. WHITNEY & COMPANY: New York, NY

Electrical/Electronic Analyst

Follow the major appliance, consumer electronic, and electronic component industries. Analyze companies and industries and evaluate stocks. Handle numerous clients such as banks, mutual funds, and insurance companies. Discuss findings, predict market trends, and advise clients on sensitive issues.

1984 - 1990

I.M.C. DIVISION OF M.R.W., INC.: Philadelphia, PA

Market Research Manager

Supervised two analysts in performing studies on the market for fixed and variable resistors in the television, computer, automotive, and other electronic markets. Forecast potential acquisitions. Chaired the Electronic Industries' Association Resistor Marketing Committee.

1980 - 1984

WOLMITE INC., Transistor Division: Waltham, MA

1982 - 1984

Market Research Manager

Identified applications and markets of various semiconductor technologies. Evaluated potential markets and monitored trends in the computer, power rectifier, television, automotive, and instrumentation markets.

1980 - 1982

Senior Engineer

Designed high-current rectifier test equipment and trained customers on rectifier applications.

EDUCATION

WESLEYAN UNIVERSITY
M.A. - Electrical Engineering

NORTHEASTERN UNIVERSITY
B.S. - Electrical Engineering

MEMBERSHIPS

IEEEE, American Society of Engineering Specialists

ERIC J. KUTCHEY, JR.
12 Candear Street
Tampa, FL 33675
(813) 555-4567; fax: (813) 555-3467 - call first

MANAGEMENT

Planned, budgeted, and managed development of products from inception through final production. Hired, developed, and supervised results-oriented professionals and technicians. Organized and coordinated teams of R&D, marketing, and market research people for key projects. Established procedures for managing and controlling projects.

TECHNICAL/SCIENTIFIC

Achieved technical and consumer objectives for innovative underarm products, facial cleansers, and hand lotions. Solved critical problems in formulating, packaging, and evaluating performance of anhydrous suspension roll-on, pump, aerosol, and squeeze spray deodorants. Supervised manufacture, microbiological safety, and efficacy testing of products. Directed research in dry skin treatment, including developing instrumental methods of evaluating product actions. Invented processes for surface coloring of gelatin capsules and spray-granulating powders. Developed electronically instrumented tablet presses and an electronic method for measuring antiperspirant activity. Created unique shampoos, rinses, shaving aids, foot sprays, contact lens solutions; plus dentifrice, antiseptic, cold, and vitamin preparations.

COMMUNICATIONS

Maintained R&D liaison with marketing, market research, advertising, legal, and regulatory agencies. Presented key accomplishment and progress reports to senior technical and business management. Handled technical training programs for sales, marketing, and advertising people and prepared comprehensive safety and efficacy manuals to obtain management clearance for sale of products. Interfaced with contract manufacturers, consulting and testing laboratories.

EMPLOYMENT

1995 - Present	CHEMICAL & METAL PRODUCTS, INC.: Tampa, FL Group Leader
1983 - 1995	JENSEN & JENSEN, INC.: Ft. Lauderdale, FL Group Leader

EDUCATION

ALBANY COLLEGE OF PHARMACY
B.S. - Pharmacy; additional courses in improving managerial skills, pharmaceutical and cosmetic engineering, aerosol technology.

DAVID NGUYEN
452 Ocean Avenue
Arlington, VA 22212
(703) 555-8742 AOL NGUDAVE

JOB TARGET

ELECTRICAL ENGINEER - Research and Development

CAPABILITIES

- Conduct R&D including design, manufacture, and testing of electrical components, equipment, and systems.
- Apply R&D findings to design new uses of equipment.
- Design manufacturing, construction, and installation procedures.
- Direct staff of engineering personnel in producing test control equipment.
- Direct test programs to insure conformity of equipment and systems to customer requirements.
- Develop schematics using CAD software.

ACHIEVEMENTS

- Designed and drafted ship/vessel electrical deck plans including power and lighting systems, fire control, and security.
- Designed, drafted, and tested telephone relay wirings, alarm, and security systems circuitry.
- Calculated projects in accord with the latest N.E. Code together with the best economic and engineering considerations.
- Designed and implemented layout of plans, sections and details of power distribution, systems, and security.
- Designed and implemented layout of H.V.A.C. wirings and control wiring diagrams.

WORK HISTORY

1994 - Present	ROSENBLUTH & STERN, INC.: Washington, DC Electrical Engineer
1989 - 1994	SMITH-ABBOT, INC.: Arlington, VA Electrical Designer
1986 - 1989	NATIONAL TELEPHONE: Washington, DC Engineering Aide

EDUCATION

1989	Catholic University: Washington, DC B.S. - Electrical Engineering

BRADLEY SHAW
331 Fort Salonga Road
Northport, NY 11687
(516) 555-2175

JOB TARGET   CONSULTING - MATERIALS SCIENCE, INSTRUMENT
APPLICATIONS OR SALES

CAPABILITIES

- Write reports using Microsoft Office and WordPerfect.
- Provide consultation to U.S. Government on contamination problems.
- Set up procedures and special techniques for the nondestructive analysis of integrated circuits, printed circuit boards, semiconductor devices, laser materials, and internal components.
- Organize and maintain analytical facilities for the characterization of metals, alloys, ceramics, polymers, plastics, fluids, and lubricants.
- Manage programs in materials and component development.
- Conduct corrosion and outgassing studies.

ACCOMPLISHMENTS

- Supervised analytical chemistry lab of six to nine graduate chemists.
- Acted as troubleshooter for equipment failure associated with aerospace and ocean systems.
- Purchased all technical equipment.
- Set up nondestructive testing procedures for failure analysis of integrated circuits.
- Conducted comparative analysis of surfactants in electroplated and anodized parts.
- Assisted in developing procedure for removing carbon inclusions from diamonds.

WORK HISTORY

1970 - Present   GAGE-WEST CORPORATION: Garden City, NY
Supervisor, Analytical Chemistry Lab

1987 - 1988   DARNELL ELECTRONICS: Bethpage, NY
Consultant

1986 - 1988   R.E.T. SURFACE CHEMICALS: Northport, NY
Consultant

EDUCATION

LONG ISLAND UNIVERSITY
Business Administration - 25 credits completed

HOFSTRA UNIVERSITY
M.A. - Microbiology/Oceanography, B.A. - Chemistry

JULIO GARCIA
766 Porter Avenue
Columbus, OH 43219
(614) 555-2334; Compuserve 56889,4366
Internet 56889.4366@Compuserve.Com

JOB TARGET PROGRAMMER

CAPABILITIES

- Program IBM PC and compatibles in OS-2 Warp and Windows 95 environments.
- Design user interface in software programs that incorporate easy-to-follow logical progression of steps.
- Program software in C, C++, Visual BASIC, Pascal, and UNIX.
- Design and produce computer-generated graphics.
- Operate DOS machines and peripherals; diagnose and fix hardware problems.
- Operate a variety of software programs including most major authoring systems, word processors, database programs, spreadsheet and graphics packages.

ACCOMPLISHMENTS

- Designed and programmed an attendance/registration database program for the Ohio School of Electronics.
- Created six utility programs that have been distributed through the Shareware network; received over two thousand registrations from satisfied users.
- Won Golden Disk Award (utilities category) for 1993.
- Established the Central Ohio PC User's Group; increased membership from 10 to 235 people in four years.
- Created and maintained an on-line 24 hour bulletin board for a PC users' group.

WORK HISTORY

1991 - present WAYLAND PLASTICS, INC.: Columbus, OH
Assistant Manager - Shipping

1988 - 1991 OHIO SCHOOL OF ELECTRONICS: Columbus, OH
Registration Clerk (work-study program)

EDUCATION

1991 OHIO SCHOOL OF ELECTRONICS: Columbus, OH

LAWRENCE F. O'TOOLE
3 Greenwald Avenue
Tumwater, WA 98502
(206) 555-6567
INTERNET-35578.2314@AOL.COM

GEOLOGY:

- Supervised and directed drilling, logging, and coring activities during well site operations.
- Evaluated, examined, and prepared drill cuttings and core samples during well site geological investigations.
- Conducted surface mapping investigations by taking field measurements of dip and strike.
- Testified numerous times before the State Oil and Gas Commissions of Texas and Louisiana.

TECHNOLOGY / HAZARDOUS WASTE:

- Certified in OSHA Safety and Health Training for hazardous waste site investigations.
- Monitored CERCLA, RCRA, SARA Title III, TSCA, and other environmental requirements and regulations.
- Proficient in the theory and application of gamma, geophysical, and resistivity logs.
- Designed and created computer programs used in the development of drilling programs.
- Utilized technical writing skills and constructed graphs and charts for government use.

WORK HISTORY

1992 - present	EXXON, USA, INC.: Tumwater, WA Geotechnical Consultant
1988 - 1992	MHQ CORPORATION: Tumwater, WA Geological Consultant
1978 - 1988	KUFACKER EXPLORATION CO.: Walla Walla, WA Area Geologist

EDUCATION

Present	Tumwater Community College Hazardous Materials Management
1978	MISSOURI SCHOOL OF MINES: Rolla, MO B.S. - Geology

MARCUS T. YARDLEY
340 Harding Place, APT. 5547
Chicago, IL 60610
(312) 555-4345; fax (312) 555-7898

Newspaper Journalism

- Provided regional political reporting for a newspaper with a circulation of 130,000.
- Covered the City of Suffolk, VA including zoning and planning boards, city council meetings, neighborhood issues.
- Wrote articles on regional issues including transportation, housing, and the economy.
- Reported on court proceedings in five suburban Chicago-area Circuit Court districts. Covered U.S. District Court proceedings.
- Reported spot coverage of police, politics, and public relations.
- Served as weekend editor, edited copy, and made daily schedule for wire-service clients.
- Covered Illinois state politics including State Legislature and local political races.
- Developed media stategy and campaigns to attract coverage of housing issues such as the Low-Income Housing Credit and other nonprofit development efforts.

Music Industry Journalism

- Developed in-depth understanding of the pop music industry.
- Wrote feature stories and articles about relationship of pop music industry politics and political culture.
- Wrote live concert and record album reviews.
- Reported on record industry news and interviewed musicians.
- Published articles in suburban *Chicago Tribune,* music industry magazines including *Catharsis* and *Jet Lag*, and political magazines.
- Founded, published and edited a music magazine, *Better Than Anything*, in Urbana, IL.

Work History

1995 - 1996   *Suffolk News Daily Press*: Suffolk, VA
Reporter

1993 - 1995   *Chicago City News* Bureau: Chicago, IL
Court Room Reporter, General Assignment Reporter

Education

1993   University of Illinois: Champaign-Urbana, IL
B.A. - Political Science

ALEXANDER MATTHEWS
21830 Korn Road
Scottsdale, AZ 85251
(602) 555-3781 office (602) 555-3534 fax - call first

JOB TARGET   Advertising Manager

CAPABILITIES

- Consult with clients, initiate sales and services, and negotiate contracts.
- Initiate, design, and orchestrate all creative points in the development of advertising campaigns utilizing a diversity of media: video, animation of all print, and computer-generated art and graphics. Proficient in Freelance, Powerpoint, and Vision.
- Organize and manage all aspects and details in the execution of the projects from start through completion. Maintain detail with Microsoft Project 4.0.
- Manage and supervise advertising and design units.
- Speak and write Spanish fluently.

ACCOMPLISHMENTS

- Organized, planned, and executed the design, schedule, and direction for over 42 catalogs, direct-mail pieces, brochures, and other print materials.
- Planned and art-directed commercial photography and video sessions for major commercial clients, television and video producers, retail catalogers and retail industry, utilizing multiformats.
- Art-directed and coordinated a multimedia campaign for an international television film series with the United States and Spain; designed the promotional package and secured $2 million in funding for this project.
- Automated the design department for Arizona Public Television with new hardware/software purchases that generated a 150% increase in production rates for an extensive client base.

WORK HISTORY

1995 - Present   Arizona Public Television: Phoenix, AZ
                   Associate Manager of Advertising Services

1990 - 1995   Desert Graphics, Inc.: Phoenix, AZ
                   Advertising Production Assistant

EDUCATION

1990   EASTERN MICHIGAN UNIVERSITY: Ypsilanti, MI
                   B.A. - Business Administration and Marketing

1984   ST. CLAIR COMMUNITY COLLEGE: Port Huron, MI
                   Commercial Art and Computer Graphics

ANGELA McGOVERN KING
338 East 70th Street
New York, NY 10018
(212) 877-5528 home (212) 663-1121 messages

WORK HISTORY

1993 - Present   DOBBS, DANE & KRONBACH, INC.: New York, NY

Media Planner

Analyze marketing objectives, formulate media strategies, and recommend best media plans for national computer software/hardware accounts. Communicate media plans in writing and direct client presentations. Responsible for $6.0 million multimedia account with heavy television as well as $4.0 million heavy print media account. Supervise one assistant planner.

Assistant Media Planner

Tabulated budget, quarterly reports, and spot television recaps and ran comparisons on database computer system. Contributed to all media-planning activities such as extensive individual market research on television usage. Participated in strenuous media department training program.

1992 - 1993   KOHENY, SHALLER, & GILBERT, INC.: New York, NY

Media Buyer

Formulated media plans for all direct marketing clients of the agency. Accounts included Fargo's Department Store credit cards. Placed advertisements in major publications and monitored responses.

1988 - 1992   STIX, SCRUGGS, & BARNEY, INC.: Chicago, IL

Media Buyer

Negotiated broadcast rates for direct marketing clients. Assisted in traffic, light production of print, casting, and production of radio and television commercials.

EDUCATION

1988   BRADLEY UNIVERSITY: Sterling, IL
B.S., Advertising

MARITA E. NICHOLS
339 Wyndham Road
Teaneck, NJ 07666
(201) 555-6001

EXPERIENCE:

EDITING

Responsible for production editing of social science textbooks for major publisher. Managed complete book production process from copy editing to printing and distribution. Successfully produced over a dozen textbooks.

WRITING

Wrote major best-selling study guides for fiction including *Anna Karenina, War and Peace, Don Quixote,* and four plays by Ibsen. Wrote introduction and recipes for widely read community cookbook.

RESEARCH

Studied, wrote, and published sets of widely distributed study materials about the lives and works of Tolstoy, Cervantes, and Ibsen. Developed and shared research techniques that cut participants' study time by 25%.

THERAPY

As psychotherapist, counseled dozens of individuals, couples, families, and groups in mental health centers. Established successful experimental methods based on Viola Spolin's theater games.

EDUCATION:

FAIRLEIGH DICKINSON UNIVERSITY
M.S. - Clinical Psychology
Wrote thesis on the use of writing as therapy for adults and children. 1990

CAROLINE STEVENS

885 Huntley Road
Charlotte, NC 28227
704-555-3388 Home   704-555-4421 Office

Created and produced HARTON magazine, the widely recognized shipping and distribution magazine of the Hart-Compton Group. With a circulation of 18,000, this highly respected publication is frequently quoted in the trade press. Developed and managed Office of Immigration Affairs for the Hart-Compton Group. Established reputation as expert in matters of immigration law and procedure.

1982 - Present	HART-COMPTON INC.: Charlotte, NC The industry leader in worldwide ocean transportation and specialty storage. Editor, HARTON Magazine

Create and produce corporate magazine for worldwide distribution. Establish content, format, and style. Direct the activities of writers, typesetters, graphic designers, photographers, and printers. Set editorial policy and objectives with senior management; report directly to Chairman and Chief Executive Officer.

1987 - Present   PUBLIC RELATIONS

Establish and administer corporate graphic standards, defining the visual style for all company communications and strengthening its public image. Produce advertisements, capabilities brochures, promotional materials, departmental manuals, special projects. Write and publish the *President's Update*, a biweekly newsletter from the president to all employees. Write, proofread, and copy-edit presentations made by senior management.

1982 - 1987   MANAGER, U.S. IMMIGRATION

Managed a complete immigration service for international employees relocating to and from the U.S. keeping fully current with prevailing laws, regulations, local practices and conditions. Recommended to top management appropriate options for recruitment and relocation of personnel depending upon visa status. Maintained liaison relationship with government and legal authorities; coordinated with in-house and outside counsel. Prepared petitions, applications, motions to the Department of Justice, State, and Labor. Saved company up to $150,000 per year in legal fees.

1977 - 1982   U.S. HOUSE OF REPRESENTATIVES: Washington, DC
                          LEGISLATIVE ASSISTANT

Researched legislation; prepared correspondence for signature; worked with committee staff in preparation for hearings; conducted casework through various agencies. Designed, wrote, and circulated congressman's quarterly newsletter to constituents.

EDUCATION

UNIVERSITY OF NORTH CAROLINA
B.A. - English/Psychology - Phi Beta Kappa

CARLTON R. RICHARDS
22 Westfield Road
Richmond, VA 23203
(804) 555-6588 (phone & fax)

PUBLIC RELATIONS

Handled customer complaints in large retail store. Organized employee/customer liaison group and represented employee views to management. Conducted several interviews with prominent sports figures for publication in local paper. Successfully negotiated language and living arrangements in Switzerland. Acted as spokesperson for college track team.

SALES

Sold merchandise in nationally known department store. Handled three times previous volume in sales. Produced high sales of six previously slow-moving items. Trained three other successful salespersons.

ACCOUNTING

Handled all bookkeeping and accounting for local retail store. Initiated and implemented computer based payroll system and created financial reports. Supervised all purchases, reducing incidental expenses by 30%.

WORK EXPERIENCE

1992 - Present   MADE IN AMERICA STORES: Richmond, VA
                  Bookkeeper

1989 - 1992   K-MART: Richmond, VA
                  Salesperson

1988 - 1989   CIBA-GEIGY CORPORATION: Richmond, VA
                  Shipping Clerk

EDUCATION

1992   UNIVERSITY OF VIRGINIA
                  B.A. - English

SPECIALTIES

Have lived nine months in Switzerland. Proficient in French reading, writing, and speaking.

JOAN TRACY
11 Breezy Point Harbor
Sarasota, FL 34236
(813) 555-1155 home; (813) 555-2674 business

EXPERIENCE:

1991 - Present   LES TROIS CYPRES SPA: Sarasota, FL

              Spa Manager

- Designed, implemented and directed a full service beauty spa.
- Escalated a two-room spa to national recognition, and tripled business within seven years. Salon was selected from several hundred by a major corporation to develop a hair and skin care line.
- Prepared for a national opening of two salons, visiting each personally to train staff and set up the entire operation.
- Consulted with advertising agencies to develop a contemporary concept of personalized skin care.
- Authored a full training manual encompassing all aspects of spa management and wrote a reference sequel for employees.
- Hosted several on-location Channel 8 TV interviews; quoted in national magazines for several photo shoots.
- Conducted highly successful seminar series for plastic surgeons and dermatologists. Spoke to groups from 50 to 1,500 with equal ease. Sought after as a speaker in the beauty care field. Researched expertise of beauty experts and hosted monthly meetings to continually upgrade staff.

1990 - 1991   GEORGETTE KLINGER, INC.: Boca Raton, FL

              Makeup Artist

- Performed wide variety of functions including makeup sales of over $500 per day, and 20 to 30 makeup applications per 12-hour day.

EDUCATION:

        International Congress Symposium: Monte Carlo
        Certification in Training Techniques - Full Service Salons

        Dale Carnegie Course
        Certified for Effective Presentation

        National Academy of Hairdressing
        Licensed Cosmetologist and Esthetician

FRASIER KARTIUK
3277 Old Mission Road
Chattanooga, TN 37411
(615) 555-7612 AOL KARTIRE

EMPLOYMENT

1985 - 1996   Halstead Tire Company: Chattanooga, TN
MANAGER / ASSISTANT MANAGER

Directed operation, selling average of $1.5M annually in wholesale/retail automobile and truck tires, and automobile repair service. Spearheaded store's growth from $.5M to $1.5M annual sales in two years through conscientious dedication and excellent customer relations. Supervised 10 employees in service and warehouse departments. Coordinated all phases of operations in sales, service, and warehouse departments.

Built team spirit and morale with employees through highly visible management and strong rapport with colleagues. Interfaced effectively with general public dealing with an average of 50 customers daily. Acknowledged by employees for fairness, sense of humor, and conscientious dedication to quality work. Achieved outstanding attendance record over 11 years.

1982 - 1985   Firestone Tire and Rubber Company: Knoxville, TN
ASSISTANT STORE MANAGER

Gained broad experience in billing, purchasing, merchandising, management, credit and collection, inventory and quality control, statistical record keeping, and light accounting.

EDUCATION

1980 - 1982   UNIVERSITY OF TENNESSEE: Knoxville, TN
Economics, Math concentration

Company/Military-sponsored training programs in personnel development and office management.

DOUGLAS I. UPTON
12 Meadows Road
Southfield, MI 48037
(313) 555-6690; (313) 555-6789 FAX

COMPUSERVE UPTON@AOL.COM

MANAGEMENT:

Responsible for day-to-day smooth operation of home office. Hired and trained personnel in selling insurance and processing claims. Reviewed activity reports for status quotas, underwriting and crediting collections to accounts. Developed sales methods leading to 60% sales increase in nine months. Reconciled commission accounts for salespersons.

SALES:

Sold insurance to 20 new major accounts in six months. Sold increased insurance to over 12 present customers. Analyzed insurance requirements for over 100 prospective clients. Supervised ten salespersons; trained them in sales techniques resulting in a 60% increase in sales.

UNDERWRITING:

Processed risks ranging from small $5,000 single engine aircraft to large multi-engine $30 million commercial jets. Increased territorial premium volume by 20%. Revised underwriting manual; developed new claims forms; set up underwriting training program.

WORK HISTORY:

1990 - Present	AERONAUTICS UNDERWRITERS: Southfield, MI
1994 - Present	Manager of Office Services
1992 - Present	Underwriter
1991 - 1992	Assistant Underwriter
1990 - 1991	Special Agent
1984 - 1990	U.S. AIR FORCE
	Pilot/Operations Officer/Squadron Commander

EDUCATION:

1985	COLLEGE OF INSURANCE
1984	STEVENS INSTITUTE OF TECHNOLOGY

MARSHA SWIFT
North Denon Street
New Orleans, LA 70183
(504) 555-6631

EXPERIENCE

1994 - Present   **GENERAL PACKAGING COMPANY**
New Orleans, LA
Technical Secretary

Handled word processing using Microsoft Office.
Composed correspondence and issued shipping forms.
Organized and maintained over 350 technical files with
accounting cross-references. Recorded incoming shipments
and prepared outgoing shipping forms for samples.

1990 - 1994   **GORMAN ENGINEERING CORP.**
New Orleans, LA
Bookkeeper

Processed accounts payable checks for real estate properties.
Paid real estate taxes, insurance premiums, and utilities for
real estate. Prepared financial statements. Organized and
submitted monthly reports. Prepaid insurance premiums.
Typed yearly financial statements for corporation.

1988   **SALVATION ARMY**
New Orleans, LA
Office Manager

Supervised office functions, including supplies purchasing,
and clerical functions. Raised $260,000 for new community
center. Set up computer systems. Designed forms,
prepared news releases, letters, and acknowledgments.
Recorded donations and pledges made by corporations,
organizations and individuals.

EDUCATION

1990   **PROFESSIONAL SCHOOL FOR BUSINESS**
New Orleans, LA
Real Estate

CAROLYN M. CARTER
113 East N Street, NE
Washington, D.C. 20009
(202) 555-6689

JOB TARGET EXECUTIVE ASSISTANT TO PRESIDENT / COO / CFO
Financial Industry

CAPABILITIES

- Create and maintain a simple, highly workable file system.
- Supervise office staff with diverse duties.
- Handle high-pressure situations and deadlines.
- Compose and prepare routine correspondence using Pagemaker and Office
- Prepare financial and other reports.
- Handle purchasing for large office.
- Handle travel and hotel arrangements utilizing Microsoft Schedule.
- Manage social as well as business correspondence.
- Handle accounting procedures on IBM or Macintosh.

ACHIEVEMENTS

- Maintained business relationships with high-level financial executives.
- Supervised staff including assistant, receptionist, steward, and wire operator.
- Assisted with daily cash reconciliation up to thousands per day for travel.
- Planned itineraries; arranged trips, including a six month world tour.
- Assisted in editing financial reports.
- Maintained business and personal calendars.
- Took and accurately transcribed dictation, including 90 page annual report.
- Arranged installation of electronic quotation equipment for 100 branch offices.
- Handled documentation to facilitate international banking arrangements for firm's top six officers.

WORK HISTORY

1991 - Present   Executive Secretary to Vice President of Finance
AZOR CORPORATION: Arlington, VA

1990 - 1991   Executive/Personal Secretary to Vice President
GENERAL SECURITIES CORPORATION: Washington, DC

1983 - 1990   Executive Secretary to Executive Vice President
JASON-WALKER, INC.: Washington, DC

EDUCATION

- S.U.N.Y. Buffalo
- BENTLEY BUSINESS SYSTEMS
- NEW YORK INSTITUTE OF FINANCE

JESSE MILANO
329 Winston Court
West Hartford, CT 06117
(203) 555-1231

JOB TARGET   Retail Store Display Designer

ENVISIONER

- Visualized innovative methods of designing and creating imaginative environments.
- Used scrap lumber and other trash collectibles to construct different display themes; developed new ways to use existing display materials.
- Designed and constructed costumes from Goodwill finds to old hospital gowns.
- Designed stage props using various-height ladders, colored filters, and back lighting.
- Completely redecorated and remolded two houses and an apartment, designing specific structures to fit designated areas.
- Designed and built bookshelves, storage systems, and bathroom interiors to effectively utilize available space.

SCOUT

- Able to assemble and create artifacts from small finds.
- Dressed an entire cast with 20 yards of muslin, dyed and fashioned for each character.
- Tore up packing crates and rebuilt them to make fences and posts to use in a display.
- Decorated an entire apartment using linoleum and wallpaper bought at garage sales. Furnished apartment by getting to know trash collectors and using their knowledge in searching for good pieces.

COORDINATOR

- Arranged new system of storing merchandise; designed inventory tracking system to prevent reordering of supplies already in stock.
- Organized a block party for 80 families; formed committee to canvass neighborhood; ordered food and drink from suppliers and arranged for food preparation; organized activities and entertainment.
- Started International Gourmet Club with rotating hostess and alternating guests.

EXPERIENCE

1981 - present   Freelance Photographer, Community Volunteer, Homemaker

1975 - 1981   Commercial Artist for department store (Gimbel's)

1972 - 1975   Assistant Artist for publishing firm (Ludden & Ludden)

JUAN RAMIREZ
1995 Barbara Street
Torrance, CA 90503
(310) 555-3233 evenings (310) 555-9989 FAX
RAMI @ AOL.COM

WORK HISTORY

1992 - present   Chief Caterer
                  J & R CATERING: Lomita, CA

                  Developed business sales that exceeded $228,000
                  annually. Contracted catering services for parties; held a
                  major account to provide catering for the Lomita Civic
                  Center. Catered many different events from picnics to
                  formal dinners for more than 3,500 persons. Managed
                  catering services for the Culver City Masonic Temple for
                  one year. Managed staff of 50; organized jobs; ordered,
                  prepared and delivered food.

1988 - 1992   Night Chef
                  INNS WAY MANAGEMENT, INC.: Seattle, WA

                  Supervised five chefs during night shift for two area
                  Radisson hotels. Received a four-star rating by the
                  American Automobile Association. Hired, trained, and
                  supervised kitchen personnel; maintained payroll
                  records; monitored performance.

1982 - 1987   Partner/Owner
                  THE GROTTO: Seattle, WA

                  Took over a failing restaurant and in three years grossed
                  over $2 million. Developed a menu specializing in Cajun
                  and Creole food.

EDUCATION

1981   PORTLAND COMMUNITY COLLEGE
                  A.S. - Applied Science in Culinary Arts

ELIZABETH HUNDHAUSEN

3375 Wacker Drive
Chicago, IL 60606
(312) 555-1218 - Messages

PURCHASING/RETAIL AND CATALOG

- Selected merchandise for retail.
- Determined price strategy and markup.
- Examined merchandise and selected colors.
- Prepared contracts with full backup data.

PRODUCT DEVELOPMENT

- Initiated changes in products to increase sales.
- Analyzed merchandise for defects in design and material to improve quality of merchandise.
- Analyzed comparative merchandise and produced reports.

ADMINISTRATION

- Coordinated, implemented, and supervised maintenance of all office records and systems using Intuit Quickbooks 3.0.
- Acted as liaison between sources and retail stores.
- Coordinated purchase orders and responded to customer complaints and service inquiries.
- Trained employees from the Buyer's Assistant Training Program.

WORK HISTORY

1984 - Present   SHORE RADNOR & COMPANY: New York, NY
                    Fashion Buying Office

1991 - Present   Buyer's Assistant

1984 - 1991   Senior Clerical Assistant

EDUCATION/TRAINING

1984   Morris Knowles High School Graduate

                    Fluent in German

MICHAEL JAMES FORDER
4468 Ellsworth Drive #232
Minneapolis, MN 55406
(612) 555-6655; COMPUSERVE 67998,4505

WORK EXPERIENCE

1993 - Present   Operations Supervisor
RYGH HEALTH CARE CENTERS: Minneapolis, MN

Supervised all functions of the Operations Department consisting of three route drivers. Purchased all inventory and established stock levels. Negotiated purchase agreements with vendors to establish best pricing and to return obsolete inventory for full credit. Developed purchasing system to reduce inventory on hand and fill back orders more efficiently. Implemented procedures for transporting hazardous wastes.

1990 - 1993   Supply, Procurement, and Distribution Technician
ST. CLAIR HOSPITAL: Minneapolis, MN

Established and maintained stock levels of medical and surgical supplies for all hospital wards, emergency room, and surgery. Checked, cleaned, and sterilized instruments used for surgery and the emergency room. Purchased and maintained inventory stock levels for the central supply department.

1982 - 1987   Radio Announcer
KSZT RADIO STATION: Minneapolis, MN

Prepared and broadcast an eight-hour radio music program consisting of hourly news, weather, and sports. Wrote and produced commercial copy for local sponsors. Designed and maintained top-40 play list from Billboard Top 100.

EDUCATION

1990   MANKATO TECHNICAL COLLEGE: Mankato, MN
A.A. - Business Administration

REGINA KAYE WILCOX
557 East 64th Street
New York, NY 10021
(212) 555-8990; AOL@ATMAN1

EXPERIENCE

1994 - Present   WORLD CONTINENTAL AIRWAYS: New York, NY
Supervisor Flight Services - Administration

- Commended for diligent efforts increasing voluntary leaves of absence, thus decreasing involuntary furloughs.
- Coordinated medical grounding/ungrounding activity and related payroll activity for 3000 New York-based Flight Attendants.
- Organize and administer flight service jet emergency training activities in a timely manner adhering to all deadlines.
- Process and authorize special leave-of-absence requests.
- Arrange and award annual vacations for New York base.
- Provide data and assistance to Personnel Supervisors and Flight Attendants concerning appropriate administrative procedures.
- Monitor Flight Attendant visa requirements.

1994   Flight Attendant

- Ensured passenger safety by complying with company and FAA requirements.
- Served as liaison between cabin crew members and cockpit crew.
- Directed scheduled food and beverage services in a timely manner.
- Conducted pre-flight briefings for flight service crew.

1992 - 1994   PALMETTO SALON: Fort Lauderdale, FL
Assistant Manager/Stylist

- Maintained loyal following of 150 clients.
- Reconciled daily receipts averaging $5000.
- Organized distribution of commissions to seven stylists.
- Purchased and logged inventory.

1991 - 1992   GREAT LOOKS SALON: Fort Lauderdale, FL
Owner/Stylist

- Raised initial capital to purchase salon.
- Created and administered employee motivational program.
- Led monthly meetings to ensure quality performance and service.

1987 - 1991   IMAGESTYLE SALON: Fort Lauderdale, FL
Manager/Stylist

- Tripled total customer base in three years.
- Doubled personal clients in one year.
- Developed advertising and promotional campaign that increased salon revenue 400% to $160,000 per year.

EDUCATION

1992   Stephenson College: Hollywood, FL
A.S. - Data Entry

MARGARET FORRESTER
1556 Appleton Drive
St. Louis, MO 63132
(314) 555-4433 Messages (314) 555-5665 FAX

JOB TARGET: CONCIERGE - HOTEL INDUSTRY

COMMUNICATIONS / HOSPITALITY

- Handled variety of clerical/social functions including reception, entertaining, and making people of diverse interests and economic status feel comfortable.
- Coordinated and oversaw two Ameritech Regional conferences that were highly acclaimed (attended by 2000 and 6000 each).
- Accustomed to accepting responsibility, delegating authority and working with people of all ages.
- Wrote surveys to elicit customer feedback; developed correspondence to enhance customer support and calculate impact of various programs.
- Coordinated many community events including Pace Setter activities.
- Participated in a wide variety of diverse activities including United Negro College Scholarship Fund, WBI Person-to-Person Friendly Visit Program, and the Juneau Village Ronald McDonald Charity.

MANAGEMENT

- Supervised 10 to 15 associates and effectively helped develop careers.
- Assisted in the creation of consumer market education recommendations and new employee orientation programs.
- Initiated and coordinated human resource programs for a broad variety of populations. Acknowledged for outstanding dedication and follow-up.
- Developed projects with attention to detail and timely, cost-effective, high-quality results.

WORK EXPERIENCE:

1966 - 1996   SOUTHWESTERN BELL TELEPHONE
Various positions, including middle management

1979 - Present   Welcome Wagon, March of Dimes, American Cancer Society
Volunteer, multiple positions

EDUCATION: Successfully completed numerous management and personal development courses.

High School Graduate/Scholarship to Nursing School

ALEX IVAN BALLISTER
33 Linden Street
Allentown, PA 18103
215-555-5465 office; 215-555-6878 fax

WORK EXPERIENCE:

1990 - Present   **BLACK & DECKER** (acquired by GE): Allentown, PA

1971 - 1990   **GENERAL ELECTRIC COMPANY**: Allentown, PA
        Housewares Manufacturing Department

1990 - Present   SENIOR MANUFACTURING PLANNER

Established work methods and work measurements. Procured
equipment to manufacture Allentown products safely at low
cost. Collaborated on setting realistic and challenging
operation goals. Cited by senior management for achieving
highest productivity goals in sixth year on the job.

Planned and established approved revisions in operations,
equipment, and tools to accommodate production schedule
changes, product mix, or design changes. Analyzed methods,
facilities, and processes leading to lower manufacturing costs.
Coordinated task forces for cost reduction.

1981 - 1990   MANUFACTURING ENGINEER

Evaluated and appraised changes to and deviations from
design, materials, and specifications. Investigated customer
complaints and recommended corrective action.

Evaluated product designs and applications. Analyzed
phototype models of housewares products. Determined
manufacturing specifications and cost projections.

1971 - 1981   LAB TECHNICIAN

Handled simple technical, analytical procedures.

EDUCATION: HIGH SCHOOL GRADUATE

RICHARD MICHALSKI
667 Binghamton Road
Bridgeport, CT 06612
(203) 555-4446, ext. 68 (203) 555-4486 fax

WORK EXPERIENCE

1973 - Present	U.S. ELECTRICAL, Div. - Hammond Electric: Bridgeport, CT

1990 - Present

AREA SALES MANAGER/ADMINISTRATION MANAGER
Direct sales and marketing responsibility for the Middle East and Africa. Make four to six sales trips per year ranging from two to three weeks per trip. Assisted in setting forecasts, administering salary planning, and implementing budgets of $2,000,000. Handle direct negotiation of contracts and projects with foreign government municipalities.

1982 - 1990

INTERNATIONAL MARKETING SERVICES MANAGER
Reported directly to Vice-President of International Sales. Managed 16 regional marketing representatives and customer service personnel. Directed and coordinated all administrative functions performed by foreign subsidiaries and offshore sales offices. Responsible for the training, performance evaluations and work load measurements of direct personnel. Established procedures and practices, and administered pricing, credit, financing, and distribution policies. Assisted Vice-President in expense control and budget development. Controlled and maintained incentive and commission policies.

1980 - 1982

PRICE ADMINISTRATOR - INTERNATIONAL
Administered pricing policies on orders, contracts and project bids to meet annual gross profit targets. Analyzed sub-product mix relative to product objectives and the effect on profit and loss. Conducted pricing studies on competitor's product, resulting in price publication changes.

1977 - 1980

SUPERVISOR - INTERNATIONAL
Supervised order entry, customer service, shipping and documentation and inside sales functions. Responsible for product training and education of all personnel.

1973 - 1977

CUSTOMER SERVICE REPRESENTATIVE - INTERNATIONAL
Performed as an inside sales person responsible for customer quotations and order entry. Administered management's policies on credit, financing, and customer claims.

MILITARY SERVICE
CONNECTICUT NATIONAL GUARD (1970-1976)

HAROLD E. SANBORNE
87 South Columbia Avenue
White Plains, NY 10604
(914) 555-8052 FAX (914) 555-8043

MANAGEMENT

- Hired telephone consultant engineers, training them in technical and interpersonal communications.
- Successfully expanded this group from three to thirty-four.
- Developed career path strategy and created charts with management for levels ranging from telephone consultant to project engineer.

TRAINING

- Trained over 150 people over ten months, including senior executives, critical care area managers, salesmen, and field engineers.
- Established task analysis and course objectives for these trainees.
- Applied critical judgment and professional competence in instructing over 85 field personnel in various locations.

ADMINISTRATION

- Handled inventory of technical education department.
- Organized information for budget and delivered to management.
- Supervised small group responsible for maintaining logistics for telephone central operations.
- Developed telephone call sheet formats that were later computerized, resulting in failure analysis reports now used nationwide.

TECHNICAL

- Responsible for instruction on mini and micro computer-controlled biomedical instrumentation.
- Developed troubleshooting procedures and charts on assigned instrumentation for customer and field service manuals.
- Served as national technical backup to service engineers on existing and developmental instrumentation.
- Performed the operational maintenance, troubleshooting, repair, retrofit, and updating of in-house production and customer education instrumentation.
- Served as quality control inspector for repair group under my supervision.

WORK HISTORY

1988 - Present	TECHNICAL PRODUCTS CORPORATION: White Plains, NY Technical Instructor

EDUCATION

Current	Westchester Community College Electrical Engineering
1988	Technician Certificate
1986	Electronics Certificate

ART MALINSKY
31 Outlook Street
Cranford, NJ 07405
(201) 555-1345

EXPERIENCE

1986 - 1996   INDUSTRIAL METAL COMPANY: Cranford, NJ

1992 - 1996   **Design Engineer**

Contributed significantly to the design and development of the firm's metal products. Put prototype products into commercial production, maintaining a budget and meeting deadlines. Designed and developed high-speed transfer presses, roll-forming machinery, assembly machinery, and associated tooling, gauges, feed mechanisms, and controls.

Led designers, detailers, and machine shop personnel on major projects dealing with both customers and vendors.

Member of the engineering center "Computer Use Committee." Responsible for the choice and research of new programming and developing custom CAD software.

1986 - 1992   **Mechanical Technician**

Debugged and modified new equipment. Successfully directed efforts to the development of new metal products.

1984 - 1986   L & R MECHANICAL LABORATORY: Wayne, NJ

Machinist and Toolmaker

Performed all facets in the making of precision tools and gauges. Experienced the programming and setup of numerical control machines.

1982 - 1984   BOWLES ENGINEERING COMPANY: Paramus, NJ

Machinist

Performed basic machining on many types of components and machines.

EDUCATION

1993 - Present   Fairleigh Dickinson University, Industrial Design
110 credits with high academic standing (3.82 out of possible 4.0).

KATHY ZIEGLER
53221 North First Street
Rosemont, PA 19010
(215) 555-6733

JOB TARGET   ORDER PROCESSING COORDINATOR

CAPABILITIES

- Handle customer contacts (walk-in, telephone, or correspondence); answer inquiries, resolve problems.
- Process mail or telephone orders.
- Key alpha and numeric data accurately and proficiently.
- Check completed invoices for accuracy; make corrections if necessary.
- Process orders and package merchandise.
- Determine fast and cost-effective shipping methods.
- Supervise order processing personnel; plan and assign work duties and monitor performance.

ACCOMPLISHMENTS

- Sorted over 800 pieces of mail and other deliveries on a daily basis for a hospital mail room; delivered mail to offices and departments.
- Collected outgoing mail; processed UPS and overnight deliveries.
- Improved efficiency of mail room by decreasing the time to package, weigh, and address outgoing packages.
- Monitored staff of three part-time student workers.
- Served over 2,000 customers in a fast-food restaurant, fulfilling orders and taking payment.

WORK HISTORY

1995 - 1996   BRYN MAWR HOSPITAL: Bryn Mawr, PA
Mail Room Clerk

1994 - 1995   BURGERS FOREVER: Ardmore, PA
Counter Attendant

EDUCATION

1995 - Present   BRYN MAWR COLLEGE
Bachelor's Program in Sociology--evenings

JAMES C. CALLAHAN
442 Walden Road
Boston, MA 02119
(617) 555-6522

JOB TARGET   Printed Circuit Designer / Checker

CAPABILITIES

- Printed circuit design and optimization
- Final schematic preparation
- Parts list derivation and generation
- Reviewing engineer input
- Board assembly and schematic checking
- Printed circuit artwork taping
- Relay logic and testing
- Cable design and fabrication

ACCOMPLISHMENTS

- Optimized circuit board designs by making modifications that increased reliability, manufacturability, heat transfer, noise reduction, and minimized signal paths.
- Increased the ease of servicing PC boards by critiquing succeeding engineering schematic until prototypes and schematics were ready for release to manufacturing as an entity.
- Generated unique library figures for different components using a CAD system in a database, resulting in PC boards designed in a sophisticated and timely manner.
- Designed and built van modifications to store luggage and allow sleeping space on long trips. Solution was a long raised rear deck easily disassembled.
- Collaborated with daily teams to design pellet boards and assemblies for Columbia IV. Team assignments included: scheduling, revising plans as needed, and problem solving.

EXPERIENCE

1991 - 1996	Senior PC Designer and Graphics Design Specialist OPTICON: Boston, MA
1982 - 1991	PC Designer SOUTHBORO CORPORATION: Boston, MA
1973 - 1982	Senior PC Designer in Modular Products Engineering FEATHERSTONE COMPUTER CONTROL: Boston, MA

EDUCATION

- Related Workshops: Basic Users Course for Opticon 870; Structural Analysis; Logic Design
- Switching Circuits; FORTRAN IV; Digital Logic; AOS
- AAS - Electronic Engineering, Boston College
- Graduated Massachusetts Radio and Television School

CHRISTOPER MAY
6711 Halub Avenue
Philadelphia, PA 18042
(215) 555-8892

WORK EXPERIENCE

UNITED PACKAGING COMPANY, Conshohocken, PA
1989 - Present

Coordinator Field Engineering

Coordinated manufacturing and packaging equipment.
Supervised records of all engineering projects - hours,
material, and total costs. Handled inventory control of
machine parts and equipment.

Completely coordinated monthly income statement of
department. Managed three machinists in workload schedule.

Technical Writer

Coordinated technical information from engineers. Organized
instruction books, catalogs, and brochures. Handled coloring,
labeling, illustrations, and minor technical writing.

Coordinated photography, making of progress report charts,
and transparencies for overhead projection and book
revisions.

Planner

Scheduled machines to work efficiently. Handled inventory
control of various raw materials - boxes and cartons.

EDUCATION

Southampton County Community College
Accounting and Data Processing

Inter-plant Courses
Electrical, heat seal, tool and die design, pulp and paper

Industrial management and technical writing courses

KEVIN JOHNSON
3362 Ponet Drive
Los Angeles, CA 90068
(213) 555-6789 AOL@NATTI

EXPERIENCE

1995 - Present   AMERICAN PACKAGING, INC.: Santa Monica, CA
Die Designer

- Responsible for design of small progressive dies to produce ends for metal cans. Participated in design of Button-Down and Stay-On Tab tab ends.
- Researched complete end die project for Indonesia, resulting in substantial savings due to prevention of manufacturing redundant and obsolete parts.
- Designed tooling for manufacture of plastic tops for Dixie Cup Division.

1993 - 1995   WATSON-EDISON COMPANY: Pacific Palisades, CA
Designer

- Designed conveyer layout for plant. Designed structural platforms and rings, floor layout for installation of presses, hopper, and other heavy equipment. Designed carbon-air batteries for use on railroads and buoys. Designed small fixtures to speed up and ease assembly line production.

1992 - 1993   AMERICAN PACKAGING, INC.: Santa Monica, CA
Design Draftsman

- Designed can-closing machine hookups to fillers; layout work on presses and dies. Designed open end detector used on can-closing machines to detect incomplete curled end seams after cans are sealed.

1983 - 1992   YARDLEY ELECTRIC CORPORATION: Los Angeles, CA
Designer

- Designed three silver-cell batteries for use in aerospace systems.
- Participated in the design of the "Hamilton Standard" battery used in the backpack of astronauts to maintain temperature in space suit.
- Illustrated technical materials and posters, most notably 30" x 40" color renderings of two Air-Zinc batteries designed for the U.S. Army Signal Corps. Also handled cover illustrations for the company pamphlet distributed at the I.R.E. show.

EDUCATION

1984 - 1985   Los Angeles Community College

1982 - 1984   Delchanty Drafting Institute

RANDALL RISSMAN
447 Christy Street
Carteret, NJ 07008
(201) 555-6744 FAX (201) 555-6785

ADMINISTRATION
Coordinated plant service activities, including installation, maintenance, and repair of equipment for a 30,000-square-foot data processing center. Developed preventive maintenance schedules and handled all follow-through. Maintained perfect OSHA compliance.

MECHANICS
Responsible for repairing and maintaining all mechanical aspects of a railroad coal-dumper, including bearing replacements, pump overhauls, and general machine repairs.

PIPEFITTING
Made extensive steam line alterations and additions following a conversion from coal to #6 oil firing of three boilers totaling 1250 horsepower. Replaced sections of 12-inch boiler headers.

ELECTRICITY
Assisted a licensed electrical contractor in installing residential and industrial services, equipment, and wiring.

STATIONARY ENGINEERING
Operated and maintained four piston valve steam engines; maintained four slide valve steam engines, and two duplex feed water pumps. Kept watch on two firetube and one watertube boilers generating 150 psi steam. Responsible for preparing this equipment for insurance inspections.

WORK HISTORY
1990 - Present   Maintenance Technician
TECHNICIANS, INC.: Metuchen, NJ

1987 - 1990   Oiler / Maintenance Machinist
NORTHERN RAILROAD: Port Reading, NJ

1985 - 1987   Electrician's Assistant
LEWIS ELECTRIC COMPANY: Port Reading, NJ

EDUCATION
1989   Middlesex County Vocational School
Blue-Seal license - Stationary Engineering

1988   Trenton State College
B.A., with honors.

SCOTT B. ANTHONY
233 Heart Avenue
Seattle, WA 98112
Home: (206) 555-4456   Work: (206) 555-1266

AUTOMOBILE SALES / SERVICE

- Handled more than 200 cars over the past 40 years. Employed as a mechanic in early career. Sold personal cars for profit after extensive use. Purchased numerous used cars at low cost and sold them all for profit.

- Supervised the maintenance and repair of 48 vehicles while in the armed services. During that time, handled truck parts replacement for 215 Army vehicles of the battalion.

TECHNICAL SERVICES

- Coordinated customer accounts for packing of coffee, nuts, and bakery products. Furnished packing information and style containers necessary for their individual products and packing procedures.

- Through knowledge of customer packing procedures was able to reduce material costs for the company. Cost savings were in excess of 25% per year.

LABORATORY TECHNICAL SERVICE

- Set up test packs using less costly materials to determine shelf life. Supervised group to conduct actual testing procedures.

- Reduced tin coating on cans when tin became expensive and in short supply through experimentation and follow-up.

WORK HISTORY

1969 - Present   ALLIED CONTAINER CORPORATION: Seattle, WA

1981 - Present   Technical Service Representative

1969 - 1981   Laboratory Technician

1969 - Present   Automobile Sales/Service (avocation)

MAR 15, 1997

TO: **GODFREY MANDELL** Executive Group Leader - Account Management Team
                TI - Business Marketing Services   555-1868, ext. 554

FROM: **SARAH PLESCHER,** Supervisor - Account Publicity and Advertising
                TI - Marketing Communications   555-1419, ext. 887

INTRODUCTION:

Jack Mitchell, our Senior Group Leader, suggested I contact you on your creative marketing services function. I understand Business Marketing Services is seeking outsourced competitive bids for direct-mail advertising, newsletter and cover feature PR writing. I have both the competencies and proven accomplishments to keep this work in-house at a lower cost to you and a higher return to your budget.

CAPABILITIES: Some of my capabilities / core competencies are:

- Extensive corporate, financial, and international PR and speech writing.
- Writing supervision on feature articles, films and film strips, brochures, presentations.
- Industrial writing - knowledge of welding products, industrial gases, superconductors.
- Achievement-oriented, focusing on creative, unique market positioning and volume sales.
- People friendly - excel in obtaining enthusiastic commitments from all constituent team members.

ACCOMPLISHMENTS: A partial list of my demonstrated results:

- Created in-house marketing-communications agency serving corporate, design automation and computer solid modeling divisions.
- Established the first true marketing function for a $100MM technology-driven corporation.
- Cut $250K from A&SP budgets while doubling programs and productivity versus previous outside agencies.
- Wrote an award winning direct mail program producing an unheard of 15% return.

RECENT TEXAS INSTRUMENTS HISTORY:

Supervisor - Account Publicity & Advertising	1994 - present
Marketing Communications	
Account Supervisor / Chief Copywriter	1991 - 1994
Product Development, Robots, Metallurgy, Geophysical Services	
Account Executive, Creative Developer	1988 - 1991
Technical Communications Division	

RECENT TRAINING / DEVELOPMENT / RECOGNITION:

Wrote 675 page text on promoting technology (1996 - Hill & Knowlton - *CyberAd)*
Three IRON AGE "best of issue" awards for ad readership

Previous work history, education / training: see attached standard resume.

APRIL 5, 1997

TO: **CHRIS McCAFFREY** Assistant Vice-President
Process/Environmental Engineering   555-2340, ext. 888

FROM: **JOSE RODRIGUEZ MONTENEGRO,** Laboratory Associate
Environmental Research Group   555-2340, ext. 32

INTRODUCTION:

Having analyzed your recent internal memo, I believe I have just the right talents to help you expand your department. My most recent assignment within this company, plus my EPA experience, put me ahead of most candidates regarding meeting environmental standards and regulations. I understand you will be working within Mexico. As I have dual citizenship with Mexico, I am also culturally connected to the thinking of key engineering companies in my native country.

CAPABILITIES: Some of my capabilities / core competencies are:

* Mineral and hazardous waste experience within a NAFTA-regulated country.
* Achieve professional growth through continuous research and extra laboratory participation.
* Extensive knowledge of EPA guidelines.
* Conduct professional studies on: environmental impact assessment, waste water treatment, soil remediation, and hazardous waste.

ACCOMPLISHMENTS: A partial list of my demonstrated results:

* Conducted remediation process for salt and petroleum contaminated soils. Work presented at the annual meeting of Alberta Oil, Sands and Research Authority, Calgary, Alberta 1994.
* Studied the environmental impact of sulphidic mine tailings from Ashanti Goldfields, Ghana; presented at the United Nations Development Program forum on mining and development, 1995.
* Analyzed polluted water samples from nuclear plants, resulting in major study and eventual roll back of nuclear output in three Colorado utilities divisions.
* Studied the novel treatment and recycling of waste water from a heavy oil production plant resulting in work being presented at 1996 International Symposium on Oil Field Chemistry.

RECENT A.B.A. ENVIROPROTEC HISTORY:

Laboratory Associate   1996 - present
Environmental Research Group

Research Associate   1993 - 1996
Environmental Research Group

RECENT TRAINING / DEVELOPMENT / LANGUAGE SKILLS:

MS in Mineral Engineering - Missouri School of Mines, Rolla, MO   1996

Fluent in Spanish, Windows 95, MS Word, FORTRAN, WordPerfect, Excel, SALT 1&2, FOWL

Previous work history, education / training: see attached standard resume.

NOV 20, 1997

TO: LEE FINLAYSON Vice-President
              MCI Employee Development & Career Competency Systems   555-3203, ext. 118

FROM: DALE SCHNEIDER, Manager
              MCI Career Education / Curriculum Design   555-3259, ext. 246

INTRODUCTION:

Since my department is reengineering, I'm contacting re-employment sources internally and externally. Frankly, the rumor mill is churning out some great leaks about your newly developing unit. I believe my track record and proven skills might fit perfectly with your employee self-directed training and education systems, particularly in the start-up phase where you're making numerous decisions on curriculum outsourcing. I've briefly outlined my capability and accomplishments below.

CAPABILITIES: Some of my capabilities / core competencies are:

- Having strong interpersonal skills as a college teacher and a corporate coach.
- Creating vision for corporate growth as it translates to individual development.
- Designing teaching tools for multi-level instruction, long and short-term.
- Team player and team organizer, able to coordinate broad spectrum of skill clusters.
- Decision-maker, able to translate to downstream staff both customer focus and corporate change.

ACCOMPLISHMENTS: A partial list of my demonstrated results:

- Organized first outplacement program in corporate finance division.
- Designed and taught process linking career and performance plans to organization development.
- Acknowledged by COO for leading successful bench marking effort for employee development.
- Originated and implemented first instructor certification program.
- Created and quality-assured $5MM ten-week sales-training program.

RECENT MCI HISTORY:

Manager   1994 - present
MCI Career Education / Curriculum Design

Training Director   1992 - 1994
MCI Career Systems / Outsourcing Education

Training Supervisor, Design Coordinator   1991 - 1992
MCI Career Systems / Outsourcing Education

RECENT TRAINING / DEVELOPMENT:

MBA started - Columbia University   Fall, 1997
Guest Speaker - American Society of Training & Development - "Core Competencies" June, 1996

Previous work history, education / training: see attached standard resume.

RICHARD BERGER
65 Braxton Road
St. Louis, MO 63130
(314) 555 - 3332 Voice (314) 555 - 5543 Fax

EDUCATION

1997   WASHINGTON UNIVERSITY: St. Louis, MO
            M.B.A. - Marketing

1987   B.S. - Industrial Engineering

JOB TARGET

            Marketing/Product Management

WORK HISTORY

1995 - 1996   WASHINGTON UNIVERSITY: St. Louis, MO
               Graduate Assistant

               Conducted a statewide survey of 750 small businesses to examine
               customer needs and wants. Coordinated in-depth interviews to identify
               improvement opportunities in customer support services. Edited
               incoming manuscripts and performed background research for a journal
               published by Washington University. Published over 25 articles in
               national journals and newsletters.

1989 - 1995   BAKER CONSULTANT GROUP: St. Louis, MO
               Management Consultant

               Consulted with consumer product, government, industrial, and
               aerospace industries. Presented work proposals, exhibited at trade
               shows, conducted telemarketing sales and surveys. Improved
               manufacturing productivity at work units in Pet Foods, Boeing,
               McDonnell-Douglas, and General Electric.

1987 - 1989   WELSH & WELSH, INC.
               Industrial Engineer

               Managed all industrial engineering activities for new products;
               functioned as liaison between production, engineering, and materials
               control. Implemented world-class manufacturing techniques, including
               just-in-time production into assembly operations. Identified production
               and quality improvements while working as a member of quality teams.

ANGELA J. FLANDERS

University of Wisconsin
137 South Lakewood Court
Madison, WI 63704
(608) 555-6565 Ext. 4431

PERMANENT ADDRESS
54876 East Saugerties Road
Saugerties, NY 12477
(914) 555-3887

EDUCATION

May 1997
UNIVERSITY OF WISCONSIN: Madison, WI
B.S. in Business Administration - Management

EXPERIENCE

Summer 1997
VERNON SYSTEMS CORPORATION: Kingston, NY
Input/Output Control Room Clerk

- Controlled data received or distributed in information systems.
- Recorded daily and monthly accounts receivable and sales input.
- Trained new permanent employees.

Summer 1996
ULSTER CO. SHERIFF'S MARINE DIV.: Kingston, NY
Secretary/Receptionist

- Opened and closed marine base.
- Compiled semiannual payroll report.
- Received incoming telephone and radio calls.
- Examined daily reports.
- Recorded marine violations.
- Trained new permanent employees.

1991 - 1995
STUDIO TAN AND NAIL SALON: Kingston, NY
Receptionist/Sales

- Opened and closed salon.
- Sold tanning packages.
- Prepared tanning programs for customers.
- Set up appointments for tanning and nails.

ACTIVITIES

- Active member of Phi Beta Lambda (business organization) 1994 - 1995.
- Attended 1996 Fall Leaders Conference, St. Louis, MO.
- Residence Hall Public Relations Director, 1 year.
- Residence Hall Floor Vice-President, 1 year.

ERICA KEISIC
223-A Van Cortlandt Park South
Bronx, NY 10463
(212) 555-4561 COMPUSERVE 65289,6789

EDUCATION

1994 - 1996   COLUMBIA BUSINESS SCHOOL: New York, NY
M.B.A. - Organizational Effectiveness - May 1996
Beta Sigma Phi; Dean's List. Named Macmannus Scholar for 1994-95
school year. President, Human Resources Management Club.

1988 - 1992   SWARTHMORE COLLEGE: Swarthmore, PA
B.A. - Biology - May, 1992
Vice President, Class of 1992. Resident Assistant for hall of 44
students. Served on two student council committees. Varsity field
hockey, basketball, and lacrosse. Photography editor, college yearbook.

MARINER EDUCATION ASSOCIATION: Woods Hole, MA
Completed marine biology and oceanography program. Spent six
weeks ashore and six weeks at sea. Elected class representative.

EXPERIENCE

Summer 1995   CITICORP: New York, NY
Corporate Human Resources Summer Intern
Created a clearinghouse of training programs offered throughout
Citicorp worldwide. Helped organize and conduct an all-day orientation
program for newly hired human resources professionals. Designed a
recruiting brochure. Devised a system for evaluating the mentor
program for new hires.

1992 - 1994   BRONX HIGH SCHOOL OF SCIENCE: Bronx, NY
High School Teacher
Taught Biology, Earth Science, Psychology. Advised 27 students. Set
up photomicrography laboratory. Implemented senior psychology
seminars. Coached lacrosse.

Summer 1993   MARINE BIOLOGY LABORATORIES: Woods Hole, MA
Research Technician
Performed laboratory and library research on marine invertebrates. Co-
authored several papers.

Summers 1987-92   SEASIDE LOBSTER HUT: Wellfleet, MA
Manager
Trained, directed and supervised 43 employees in a busy resort area
restaurant. Responsible for public relations, general organization,
purchasing supplies, and monitoring food quality.

TIMOTHY URICH
221 Mifflin Street
Madison, WI 53703
(608) 555-6755   INTERNET 45638.8992@AOL.COM

EDUCATION

1996   University of Wisconsin: Madison, WI
              B.A. - Communication Arts

JOB TARGET   Video Production

CAPABILITIES

- Direct productions; tape and edit using super-8 film and 1/4" videotape.
- Operate TV cameras, video control console, and audio equipment.
- Monitor on-air programs to ensure technical quality of broadcasts.
- Operate sound-mixing board to control output of voices, sound effects, and music.

ACCOMPLISHMENTS

- Assisted in preparation and striking of camera equipment on set of MTV music video; transported film between camera operators and film loaders.
- Performed grip functions on video commercial for Miller Brewing Company; operated various fog and light equipment and routed electrical hookups.
- Hosted weekly three-hour program for campus radio station.
- Produced audio commercials and print advertisements for radio station; created materials using various mixers, signal processors, and taping equipment.
- Wrote and recorded motivational song for national footwear company.

WORK HISTORY

1992 - 1996   WLHA-FM: Madison, WI
              Program Host/Disc Jockey

1994   JOHN ROACH PROJECTS: Madison, WI
              Grip

1992 - 1994   TAMARACK APARTMENTS: Madison, WI
              Resident Manager

RUSSELL BABB
446 Russell Avenue
Bridgeport, CT 06606
(203) 555-2315; FAX (203) 555-8675
AOL@BABB

EDUCATION

1996   University of Bridgeport
               B.A. in Communications Arts

JOB TARGET   BOOKING AGENT

CAPABILITIES

- Create, develop, and manage jazz and rock groups.
- Develop and implement well-planned budgets and schedules for bands.
- Scout talent for purpose of creating new groups.
- Establish and direct showcase presentations to expose new talent to the public.
- Write press releases and album covers.
- Negotiate fees.

ACCOMPLISHMENTS

- Promoted five concerts in 2000 seat auditorium for college audiences.
- Created and managed two progressive jazz groups that traveled nine states in 60 days.
- Supervised spring concert series featuring new talent and attended by over 1200 students.
- Wrote numerous reviews on new album releases for college newspapers.
- Booked jazz bands on several campuses and in local clubs.

WORK HISTORY

1995 - 1996   Chair, Concert Committee
                University of Bridgeport

1994 - 1995   Music Critic
                The Student Chronicle, University of Bridgeport Newspaper

1993 - 1994   Manager/Agent
                The Brothers Three/The Music Students

CARL GUENDEL
45 Randall Avenue
Madison, WI 53704
(608) 555-6604 COMPUSERVE 34435,5679

EDUCATION

1996   UNIVERSITY OF WISCONSIN
                B.A. - Journalism

WRITING

- Wrote 20 articles for the sports section of college newspaper.
- Wrote and sold greeting cards for charity, earning $600.
- Served as assistant editor of the sports section of college newspaper.
- Wrote sports editorials for the final edition of *The Badger News* - school newspaper.

SPORTS

- Played four years college basketball.
- Nominated "Player of the Year" in state college basketball.
- Coached high school basketball players at summer clinic.

COMMUNICATION / RADIO / VIDEO

- Announced live broadcasts of football games on college radio.
- Wrote and delivered nightly news for radio on football weekends.
- Assisted in developing basketball training via video.
- Delivered sports promotional spots on local college radio station.

WORK HISTORY

1994 - 1996   BADGER NEWS, University of Wisconsin: Madison, WI
                Assistant Editor / Sports Writer

1993 - 1994   BADGER RADIO, University of Wisconsin: Madison, WI
                Radio Sports Announcer

1992 - 1993   CAYUGA BASKETBALL CLINIC: Green Bay, WI
                Coach and Instructor

MARSHA COOK
664 Drexal Drive
Pitman, NJ
(609) 555-1150 AOL COOKBORO

EDUCATION:
1996

B.A. - JOURNALISM / COMMUNICATIONS
Glasboro State College, Glasboro, NJ

WRITING:

- Wrote four full page essays on controversial and political issues for college yearbook.
- Researched and wrote over 50 birth announcements for daily countywide newspaper.
- Reported on local political meetings for daily newspaper.
- Reported on pertinent college issues for college newspaper.

EDITING:

- Edited over a dozen newspaper articles on local events.
- Assisted in making all editorial decisions for college yearbook, which won second place in national competition.
- Selected and edited all copy for yearbook.
- Insured accuracy of all information for college freshman general information guide.

MANAGING:

- Selected and hired photographers, and managed the scheduling of all senior class photo sessions.
- Coordinated photographic shootings between five photographers with 143 groups and 203 events.
- Oversaw and approved design and layout of yearbook for two years.
- Coordinated and designed freshman orientation handbook.

PHOTOGRAPHY:

- Shoot pictures of local events and groups for daily paper.
- Shot and selected photos for a variety of college publications.

EXPERIENCE:
1993 - 1996

Yearbook Staff - Glasboro State College
Editor of SHADOW, Freshman Orientation Handbook
Assistant Editor of IMAGE, College Yearbook

1993 - 1995

Writer / Editor, Local Events
MAINLINE TIMES: Vineland, NJ

1992 - 1993

Writer, Announcements
BORO NEWS: Glasboro, NJ

STEFAN HENRIKKSEN
Purdue University
Windsor Halls, Box 356
West Lafayette, IN 47907
(317) 555-6767, EXT 66

EDUCATION

1997   PURDUE UNIVERSITY
                B.A. - Psychology
                Pertinent Courses: Advanced Statistical Analysis
                Experimental Psychology

Spring 1995   STANFORD UNIVERSITY
                Business School
                Semester study with pertinent courses in Industrial/Organizational
                Psychology, Human Resources, Management, Human Factors in the
                Work Environment; independent research on levels of moral
                development in group decision making.

EMPLOYMENT

1994 - Present Research Assistant - Psychology Department
                PURDUE UNIVERSITY: Lafayette, IN

                Coordinate experiments for a professional research data collection.
                Schedule experiments, as well as running subjects through paradigms.
                Analyze data of preliminary findings via computer designed
                spreadsheets. Train other assistants on procedures for running
                experiments.

1994   Summer Intern - Human Resources Department

                ALLIED SIGNAL CORPORATION: Morristown, NJ
                Analyzed data concerning problems with the performance evaluation
                system and generated solutions. Developed feedback information on the
                performance evaluation system for employees. Experienced the various
                aspects of human resources management (i.e., personnel, compensation,
                employee evaluation). Acquired knowledge of corporate relations and
                recruiting procedures.

ACTIVITIES

- Since 1993 - founder, counselor, and budget coordinator of the
  Purdue University Peer Counseling and Referral Service.

- Anchor for Purdue University's television station.

LAURA GREGSON
352 Kingsbury Rd.
Bridgeport, CT 06610
(203) 555-6211

EDUCATION

1996   Masters - Education
                 University of Bridgeport: Bridgeport, CT

1994   B.A. - Psychology / Spanish
                 University of Connecticut: Storrs, CT

JOB TARGET

To teach Spanish in a Grade 7-12 public school environment. To teach and coach after-school sports.

TEACHING EXPERIENCE

- Substitute - taught in all academic areas.
- Taught tennis lessons to youths, adults.
- Volunteered with handicapped children / Children's Hospital.
- Organized children's activities; served as teacher's aide, Bridgeport, Connecticut summer school program.
- Led Catholic retreat weekend discussions with adults, teens.

SPANISH TRAINING / TEACHING

- Taught Spanish on all ability levels.
- Tutored Bridgeport H.S. students in Spanish.
- Studied at University of Granada, Granada, Spain speaking only Spanish, living with local family.

SPORTS SKILLS / AWARDS / EXPERIENCE

- Achieved #1 in both Singles / Doubles Varsity Tennis Team.
- Ranked #3 in Big East Tennis; #2 in state of Connecticut.
- High School: 1) elected Captain - varsity volleyball / tennis teams.
  2) named all-prep American athlete.
- Organized children's and adults' tennis program.

AFFILIATIONS

1995 - Present   BRIDGEPORT PUBLIC SCHOOLS: Bridgeport, CT
                 Intern / Athletic Coach

1990 - Present   LAWNDALE COUNTRY CLUB: Bridgeport, CT
                 Head Tennis Pro / Assistant Tennis Pro

1985 - 1989   Bridgeport Town Recreation Program: Bridgeport, CT
                 Bridgeport Summer School Program

WILLIAM FLOYD
2 Front Street #5R
Cedar Rapids, IA 52402
(319) 555-2249 AOL@WILFLOY

EDUCATION

1996   IOWA STATE UNIVERSITY: Cedar Rapids, IA
              B.A. - Communication Arts

JOB TARGET   SALES REPRESENTATIVE

CAPABILITIES

- Sell and promote a variety of products to individuals or companies on a cold-call basis.
- Establish customer base in a familiar or unfamiliar territory within a short period of time.
- Instruct and train new employees.
- Exhibit leadership and motivational abilities.
- Communicate effectively with people in a sales and customer-relations atmosphere.
- Work on IBM PC or Macintosh computers, operate word-processing, database, and spreadsheet programs.

ACCOMPLISHMENTS

- Sold educational books on a door-to-door basis; placed orders, handled cash, and delivered items. Grossed $7,600 in sales in two-month period.
- Ranked 18th nationally out of more than 2,000 first year dealers.
- Won Gold Seal Award for dealer who averaged 80-hour work week.
- Sold/rented water-treatment systems to homeowners and commercial businesses.
- Contacted business leaders throughout Iowa as a part of marketing services of the International Business Club to promote cooperation and fellowship between Iowa and foreign businesses.

WORK HISTORY

1992 - present   CLEARWATER SYSTEMS, INC.: Cedar Rapids, IA
                 Salesperson/Service Representative

1994   C.J.'S RESTAURANT: Cedar Rapids, IA
                 Waiter

1992 - 1993   SOUTHERN PUBLISHING CO.: Atlanta, GA
                 Salesperson

CARTER B. SIMPSON
446 Berkeley Drive
Syracuse, NY 13210
(315) 555-7332 AOL@GOCART3

EDUCATION

1996   SYRACUSE UNIVERSITY
            B.A. - Urban Studies

JOB TARGET

RESEARCH ASSISTANT WITH AN URBAN / REGIONAL
PLANNING FIRM

CAPABILITIES

- Write complete and detailed research reports.
- Edit written materials for content and grammar.
- Work well under pressure to meet deadlines.
- Communicate effectively with librarians and others
  required to support research work.
- Read and summarize detailed or dense material.
- Type reports, memos, and letters on IBM P.C. and Mac.
- Receive and carry out complicated instructions and tasks.
- Sketch and draw charts and other visual materials required
  to supplement explanatory text.

ACHIEVEMENTS

- Edited college political magazine and wrote over a dozen
  articles on pertinent and controversial social issues.
- Successfully researched background material for textbook
  on urban economics written by Professor Alfred
  Hinderman.
- Won Senior prize for essay on crime in urban ghettos.
- Maintained A minus average throughout college career.

WORK HISTORY

1994 - Present   SYRACUSE UNIVERSITY DORMITORY COUNCIL
                  Newspaper Business Manager / Newspaper Deliverer

1995 - Present   PROFESSOR ALFRED HINDERMAN
                  Research Assistant

1994 - 1995   SYRACUSE DEMOCRATIC COMMITTEE
                  Campaign Worker

1993 - 1995   KARLOFF CONSTRUCTION
                  Laborer

TERENCE HANRATTY
55889 Barton Way
Chattanooga, TN 37415
(615) 555-3792; Email - AOL@ RATTY9

EDUCATION

B.A. - Sociology / Political Science - 1997
DREXEL UNIVERSITY: Philadelphia, PA

JOB TARGET   ADMINISTRATIVE ASSISTANT - SOCIAL SERVICES

CAPABILITIES

- Good analytic and planning skills.
- Proficient in PC and Mac software applications.
- Clerical abilities ranging from typing 70 wpm to fast notehand.
- Able to show compassion and understanding.
- Work with patience and focus under pressure.
- Good telephone manner.
- Work well with statistics and complex reports.

ACHIEVEMENTS

- Completed 600 five-page data collection for the U.S. Census Bureau in 45 days.
- Handled cash receipts and customer sales for a small retail shop.
- Collected and analyzed data for a U.S. presidential campaign headquarters.
- Assisted in all clerical duties of a presidential campaign headquarters.
- Canvassed 1000 homes over a 60-day period.
- Aided a human rights organization in focusing public policy through letter-writing and issues education.
- Assisted this organization in fundraising activities and petition campaigns.

WORK EXPERIENCE

1996	Howard Davies - U.S. Presidential Campaign Clerk
1994	Amnesty International Clerk
Spring 1992	U.S. Census Bureau: Administrative Assistant

SYLVIA ANNETTE CORLEY
214 Lower Lake Road
Hartford, CT 06467
(203) 555-7780; (203) 555-2400 messages

MANAGEMENT / COMMUNITY SERVICE:

Located suitable housing and employment for retarded and handicapped individuals. Networked extensively in community with employers. Referred clients to specialized skill classes to upgrade daily functioning. Created small group homes in the community where five or six handicapped people could live independently. Investigated communities where group homes could be developed, and identified municipal services available, with special attention to convenience, recreational facilities, shopping, and hospitals. Played an instrumental role in educating public to accept group homes.

COUNSELING / INSTRUCTION:

Counseled individuals in one-on-one and group settings. Assessed cases to determine appropriate placement. Evaluated clients regarding individual capabilities, housing needs and general living patterns. Established a workable program with clients. Advised individuals regarding their entitled benefits, referring them to direct sources of service. Provided follow-up services to outreach workers.

Taught braille to elderly convalescent home patients. Counseled elderly individuals with personal problems and assisted in grooming the aged.

Certified in CPR and participate as active member of Gerontology Society, National Rehabilitation Association and American Council of the Blind.

Travel independently with a guide dog.

WORK HISTORY:

1988 - Present	Self-employed - Private Practice Specializing in individual therapy & hypnosis.: Hartford, CT
1986 - 1987	Case Manager/Counselor CENTER FOR INDEPENDENT LIVING: Westport, CT
1984 - 1985	Research Survey Worker CT ASSOCIATION OF RETARDED CITIZENS: Westport, CT

EDUCATION:

1983	FAIRFIELD UNIVERSITY: Fairfield, CT M.S. - Concentration in Gerontology
1988 - 1989	In cooperation with Dr. Phillip Hanes: New Haven, CT Certification - Hypnotherapy

MADELINE JONES
355 North End Drive
Bethel, KY 05394
(217) 555-7741

SALES/FUND RAISING

- Sold Avon Products to over 500 private clients, grossing $36,000 in sales in one year.
- Increased Saturday sales in women's clothing boutique by 30% in six months.
- Raised over $700,000 for the American Heart Association through a Bike-a-Thon.

MANAGING

- Planned and coordinated all details in producing Bike-a-Thon.
- Oversaw promotional activities for Bike-a-Thon.
- Managed small boutique in owner/manager's absence.

SUPERVISING

- Supervised a staff of five volunteers for the American Heart Association.
- Supervised all activities of ten Cub Scouts for two years.
- Managed group of 75 Cub Scouts and seven volunteer adults on weekend district-wide camping trip.

WORK EXPERIENCE

1988 - Present	THREE RIVERS' BOUTIQUE Sales - Part-time
1984 - 1990	AVON Sales Representative
1982 - 1984	AMERICAN HEART ASSOCIATION Manager of Bike-a-Thon
1980 - 1982	BOY SCOUTS OF AMERICA Den Mother - Troop 405

EDUCATION

1989	Bethel Community College: Bethel, KY Courses in Business Management

HOWARD BUCKINGHAM
531 North River Road
Fargo, ND 58102
Office: (701) 555-9452 Home: (701) 555-5217
Fax: (701) 555-5218

WORK HISTORY

1995 - Present	PLAINS CONSTRUCTION: Fargo, ND President
1972 - 1995	SOUTER CONSTRUCTION COMPANY: Fargo, ND
1982 - 1995	Executive Vice President, Secretary/Treasurer
1977 - 1982	Treasurer, Assistant Treasurer
1972 - 1977	Accounting Supervisor, Accountant

ACCOMPLISHMENTS

- Joined Souter in 1972 when it was doing $6 million in volume. Purchased shares in 1986 when the volume was $16 million and grew it to $36 million by 1995.

- Developed a reputation as one of the premier Fargo contracting companies known for its high quality, reasonable cost projects.

- Contracts ranged from small renovations to a $20-million plus project.

- Scope of services included construction management, designing-building, and negotiating and bidding general construction.

- Had primary responsibility for the company's financial affairs, dealing with three financial institutions. Negotiated seven-figure bank lines of credit and mortgages. Banking relations were such that security requirements were not increased during periods of losses.

- Purchased and managed all corporate insurance and surety bonds. Achieved one of the lowest ratings in the Fargo area for a construction company on Workers Compensation, business auto, general and excess liability. Reduced insurance costs by approximately 30% by implementing a safety program.

- Designed and implemented a highly sophisticated financial information system that included detailed project accounting.

- Had key responsibility for establishing the direction of the company and providing daily management.

EDUCATION

Notre Dame University: South Bend, IN
B.S.B.A - Accounting

JUSTINE MELVIN
356 East 68 Street
New York, NY 10022
(212) 555-3451 FAX (212) 555-3456 - AOL@JUSTEL

SUMMARY OF ACCOMPLISHMENTS

- Co-produced managers' leadership development program for General Teledyne in October, 1995.
- Former partner/owner of Career Dynamics, Inc.
- Partner for twelve years to noted career development expert.
- Published in "Working Woman" magazine in 1993 and 1996 four articles on resume writing and how to survive being fired.
- Led over 200 workshops in outplacement and early retirement for employees ranging in levels from blue collar to senior executives.
- Successfully counseled over 150 individual job-seekers in private custom-designed sessions. Emphasis on women and entrepreneurs.
- Lecturer at over forty college campuses on job-finding techniques and philosophy.
- Edited and test-marketed over sixteen career-related programs in ten years with Career Dynamics, Inc.
- Trained numerous workshop leaders in the U.S.A. and Europe to deliver various career-related programs.

CLIENT COMPANY LIST (PARTIAL)

General Teledyne
Goodyear Tire & Rubber
Colgate-Palmolive
Kodak
Polaroid
New York Life Insurance Company
AT&T
Nynex
Bell Atlantic

MEMBERSHIPS

ASTD - American Society of Training & Development
CPI - Career Partners International

AWARDS

National Society of Women Business Owners 1996 Golden World

MELISSA WELCH
2677 Linden Street PH-B
Milwaukee, WI 53209
(414) 555-3244 home (414) 555-2500 office

TARGETED WORK
COMMUNITY RELATIONS / PROGRAM DEVELOPMENT

ACCOMPLISHMENTS / SPECIAL KNOWLEDGE

- Developed innovative program planning and community contact including: setting objectives, scope and sequence, designing resource retrieval systems, promotional slides, brochures; enlisting community advisory council, project consultant and on-site mentors.
- Maintained and updated records, wrote staff reports, and news press releases, enlisting and using feedback. Determined timeline and budgets. Selected materials and equipment, orienting visitors and convention delegates in program designs; handled in-house staff training stimulating performance and involvement.
- Respond sensitively to clients' needs, acting decisively, delegating as needed and performing with high energy; work in self-directive fashion with diverse groups as a team member; oriented to problem-solving; adaptable to changing circumstances; empathetic, caring, tactful, warm, ethical, inspiring public speaker, instilling enthusiasm and interest; strong abilities in business marketing and negotiating; adept writer; sensitive to the arts.

EXPERIENCE

1993 - present   Counselor / Consultant - Private Practice - Milwaukee

1993 - present   Instructor - St. Stephen's College: Milwaukee

1988 - present   Vice President - Board of Directors, Karen Horney Ctr.: Milwaukee

1991 - present   Published author in psychology; public speaker to business groups

1988 - 1993   Career Development Counselor - Milwaukee Public Schools

1983 - 1988   Board Member - Milwaukee Board of Realtors
                      Adult Education Instructor - Allied Realtors

1973 - 1983   Social Studies Instructor / Guidance - Milwaukee Public Schools

EDUCATION

1975   M.S. - Educational Psychology, Guidance and Counseling
                      University of Wisconsin

1973   B.A. - Social Studies
                      Regis College: Kansas City, MO

                      Wisconsin Professional Counselor License

FRANCIS X. GIBBONS, III
4437 Orchard Hill Road
Boston, MA 02130
(617) 555-6441 FAX (617) 555-6455
INTERNET 24450.1786 @ COMPUSERVE.COM

1987 - Present   SALES REPRESENTATIVE, SELF-EMPLOYED

- Sought out and represented leading manufacturers of women's accessories in moderate and higher price ranges and achieved sales volume of $1.7 million.
- Developed extensive experience in working with large accounts and participating in trade shows, market weeks, and other marketing activities.
- Provided full range of sales services including telemarketing, direct sales, helping customers obtain credit lines from manufacturers, leading in-store seminars, performing in-store servicing and stock counts, following up on order deliveries, and solving a wide variety of problems.
- Rented, designed, and maintained a dynamic, beautifully furnished and decorated, highly organized Boston showroom.
- Increased sales of a single product to IP Jenner from $16,000 to $350,000.
- Convinced Hospitality Hosts, Inc., to be their representative in New England. Opened 200 accounts and sold over $375,000 worth of product in the first year in a territory in which they had no accounts.
- Maintained a sales volume over $850,000 for Lowell Bros. & Co., Inc., the largest glove manufacturer in the country. Opened two new accounts for them that totaled 360 branch stores.
- Represented Heilbron, Inc., a major umbrella resource. Sold umbrellas to 60 new accounts in six months, exceeding the output of every other sales rep.
- Recognized niche opportunity in jewelry sales and created new business.
- Contributed unusual time, energy, and financial resources beyond what is normally expected of a sales representative.
- Developed and maintained effective partnership with my wife in marketing and managing the business.

EDUCATION

1987   BOSTON UNIVERSITY: Boston, MA
B. S. - Economics, Summa Cum Laude

Further Reading and Computing

CAREER AND JOB BOOKS

Other Books by Tom Jackson

Perfect Resume Strategies. The ultimate companion to *The New Perfect Resume.* *Strategies* is a resume catalog along with real-life case histories and cover-letter excerpts. Includes advice from over twenty-five career counselors nationwide. Tom Jackson and Ellen Jackson, Doubleday, 1992.

The Perfect Job Search. A complete guide to organizing a job search, containing 128 strategies to meet everyday and uncommon obstacles. Tom Jackson, Doubleday, 1992.

Power Letter Express. A quick-read 86-page booklet with a simple guide to writing job-winning letters. Tom Jackson and Bill Buckingham, Random House, 1994.

Resume Express. An easy-to-read 100-page handbook with simple exercises and twenty-three sample resumes. Tom Jackson and Bill Buckingham, Random House, 1993.

Interview Express. An easy-to-read 85-page handbook you can pop in your pocket or purse and review on your way to an interview. Tom Jackson and Bill Buckingham, Random House, 1993.

Not Just Another Job. An outstanding rewrite of Tom Jackson's breakthrough first book, *The Hidden Job Market.* Tom Jackson, Random House, 1992.

Guerrilla Tactics in the New Job Market. Contains excellent exercises for translating skills and interests into meaningful job and career targets. Tom Jackson, Bantam Books, rev. ed., 1990.

Software by Tom Jackson

The Perfect Resume. A best-selling database resume program designed for Windows 95, Windows 3.1, and Macintosh. In CD-ROM, with on-line video advice on 50 different topics and over 150 resume samples. From Davidson and Associates, 1995.

Career Planning

101 Careers: A Guide to the Fastest Growing Opportunities. A listing of the 101 best-paying occupation prospects of the 1990s. Based on research by the Bureau of Labor Statistics, recent surveys, and information compiled by representative organizations in the various professions and specialties. This book shows the occupational areas that will have the fastest growth in the next decade. Michael Harkavy, John Wiley & Sons, 1990.

The Lotus and the Pool. This is a holistic approach to career development involving the wisdom of the unconscious—expressed in dreams, symbols, personal myths, intuitions, and memories—as well as the analytical skills needed to set goals and plan strategies. Hilda Lee Dail, Shambhala, 1989.

Do What You Love, the Money Will Follow: Discovering Your Right Livelihood. A popular book becoming a classic. A step-by-step guide to finding the "work" that expresses and fulfills your needs, talents, and passions. Marsha Sinetar, Dell Publishing, 1986.

Job Search/Targeting

The 1996 What Color Is Your Parachute? Richard Bolles's bible for job hunters and career changers. Substantially updated annually for 24 years and not scheduled to halt as of now. Richard Nelson Bolles, Ten Speed Press, 1996.

Getting a Job After 50. Realistic, age-specific advice for redirecting your career or resuming it after retirement. Strong sections on age discrimination and myths/realities. John S. Morgan, Liberty Hall Press, 1990.

Is Your "Net" Working? A Complete Guide to Building Contacts and Career Visibility. Contains practical information and advice on how to develop strong networking skills and determine whether your current networking techniques measure up. Anne Boe and Bettie B. Youngs, John Wiley & Sons, 1989.

Assessments

The Career Discovery Project. Comprehensive, self-scoring, self-paced personal career profile including style, motivation, skills, internal barriers and development needs. Gerald M. Sturman, Ph.D., Doubleday, 1993.

Your Hidden Skills. Describes a method for identifying the skills you already have but are not fully aware of. Twelve steps help you develop a pattern of your key talents plus solid proof that you already use them effectively. Henry C. Pearson, Moury Press, 1981.

In Transition. Prescribes rigorous self-assessment leading to career planning, debunks conventional wisdom, and tells it like it is. Mary L. Burton, Richard A. Wedemeyer, 1992.

Wishcraft: How to Get What You Really Want. Includes exercises to discover strengths and skills, turn fears and negative feelings into positive tools, diagram the path to your goal and map out target dates for meeting it, chart daily progress, create support networks of contacts and sources, using a buddy system to get you on track. Barbara Sher, Ballantine Books, 1979.

Interviews

Marketing Yourself. The Catalyst Women's Guide to successful interviews and resumes. Catalyst Staff, Bantam Books, 1981.

The Five Minute Interview. Assertive intervention techniques for taking control of the interview and positioning yourself as the best candidate. Scores of sample interview questions are a bonus. Richard Beatty, John Wiley & Sons, 1986.

The Job Interview. A substantive booklet accompanies solid interviewing tips on two cassettes—useful in car on way to the interview. Sullivan/Lee Industries, 1989.

Personal Growth and Development

When Smart People Fail. Focus is on career failure. Looks at the process of coping with setbacks and taking advantage of options. Outlines the phases of career failure and the nine most common reasons. Carol Hyatt and Linda Gottlieb, Penguin Group, 1980.

Negotiation: The Art of Getting What You Want. A guide on how to negotiate for what you want. Michael Schatzki and Wayne R. Coffy, W. W. Norton, 1981 (Dutton original).

A Whack on the Side of the Head: How to Unlock Your Mind for Innovation. Expanding your own creativity. Roger Van Oech, Warner Books, 1983.

Communication

Are You Communicating? You Can't Manage Without It. Focuses on the people skills useful in getting ahead in the Information Age. Deals with conversation, establishing rapport, making the most of meetings, developing sparkling presentations, writing stronger memos, proposals and letters, and using vigorous language. Donald Walton, McGraw-Hill, 1991.

200 Letters for Job Hunters. Resource for rusty or uninspired letter writers. Samples cover possible situations and purposes, from approaching the company of your dreams to expressing regret after turndown. William S. Frank, Ten Speed Press, 1990.

The New Well-Tempered Sentence. Amusing, useful, and painless book that teaches you everything you want and need to know about punctuation. Karen Elizabeth Gordon, Ticknor & Fields, revised and expanded, 1993.

The 29 Most Common Writing Mistakes and How to Avoid Them. Emphasizes slanting your writing for a specific audience, using strong verbs rather than depending on adjectives, avoiding editing while writing, and sticking to your theme. Judy Delton, Writer's Digest Books, 1985.

Resources

The World Future Society. Nonprofit organization offering magazines, books, workshops, etc., dealing with future work and life.

National Directory of Addresses and Telephone Numbers. The 1,000 most-in-demand toll-free numbers. Concord Reference Books, Kirkland, Wash.

Dictionary of Holland Occupational Codes. 500 pages contain a comprehensive cross-index of Holland's RAISEC codes with 12,000 occupations from the *Dictionary of Occupational Titles.* Also contains a description of the theoretical and technical origins of the work as well as a detailed bibliography of materials on occupational research and applications. Gary D. Gottfredson, John L. Holland, and Deborah Kimiko Ogawa, Consulting Psychologists Press, 1982.

Business Periodicals Index. A subject index to business magazines and newspapers, available in business libraries.

Consumer Magazines SRDS. Directory of consumer magazines covering every hobby, interest, and age group. Standard Rate & Data Service.

New Product/New Business Digest. Lists over 500 unique, newly developed products/processes. Business Growth Services.

Index to Legal Periodicals. A guide to recent articles on business and franchise law.

GENERAL READING

Covey, Stephen. *The Seven Habits of Highly Effective People.* Simon & Schuster, 1989.

Cox, Alan. *Straight Talk for Monday Morning.* John Wiley & Sons, 1990.

Davidow, William H., and Malone, Michael S. *The Virtual Corporation.* Harper-Business Publishers, 1992.

DeBono, Edward. *Handbook for the Positive Revolution.* Viking Press, 1991.

Deep, Sam, and Sussman, Lyle. *Smart Moves.* Addison Wesley Publishers, 1990.

Drucker, Peter F. "The Age of Social Transformation." *Atlantic Monthly,* October 1994.

Everett, Melissa. *Making a Living While Making a Difference.* Bantam Books, 1995.

Fisher, Roger; Ury, William; and Patton, Bruce. *Getting to Yes.* Penguin Books, 1981, 1991.

Handy, Charles. *The Age of Paradox.* Random House, 1993.

Katzenbach, Jon R., and Smith, Douglas K. *The Wisdom of Teams.* HarperBusiness Publishers, 1994.

Kotter, John P. *The New Rules.* The Free Press Publishers, 1995.

McKay, Harvey. *Beware the Naked Man Who Offers You His Shirt.* William Morrow, 1990.

Naisbitt, John. *Global Paradox.* Avon Books, 1995.

Negroponte, Nicholas. *being digital.* Alfred A. Knopf, 1995.

Peters, Tom. *The Pursuit of Wow.* Vintage Books, 1994.

"Rethinking Work." *BusinessWeek,* October 17, 1994.

Schumacher, E. F. *A Guide for the Perplexed.* Harper & Row, 1977.

Senge, Peter. *The Fifth Discipline.* Doubleday Currency, 1990.

Stoll, Clifford. *Silicon Snake Oil.* Doubleday, 1992.

Tannen, Deborah. *Talking from Nine to Five.* William Morrow, 1994.

Toffler, Alvin, and Toffler, Heidi. *Creating a New Civilization.* Turner Publishing, 1995.

Walker, Brian Browne. *The Crazy Dog Guide to Happier Work.* Fireside, 1993.

Watts, Alan W. *The Wisdom of Insecurity.* Vintage Books, 1951.

Order Today Toll Free 1-800-233-6460

NOW: THE RESUME THAT KEEPS ON WORKING FOR YOU

The Perfect Resume Computer Kit ™

You now own the book that will help you produce a resume to present your best strengths and unique experiences to potential employers. Here's a way to take your perfect resume one step further. The Perfect Resume Computer Kit (IBM PC & Compatibles, or Macintosh CD-ROM), created by Tom Jackson and Bill Buckingham, combines the exercises and vocabularies of the book with the power of the computer to maximize the impact of your resume. It is so easy to use even non-typists can create a professionally designed resume. You can easily create a library of resumes, and update your information anytime you want.

☐ Macintosh & Windows CD-ROM (includes Resume Builder, Power Letters, Job Search Manager, and Tom Jackson's On-line Video Advice) **$59.95**
☐ Windows Version - 3.5" disks (includes Resume Builder, Power Letters, Job Search Manager) **$49.95**
☐ DOS Version (includes Resume Builder and Career Consultant modules)................................ **$39.95**

Resume Express ™

Resume Express (DOS) is a fast and easy way to assemble and print your resume. This one-disk program is best if you already have targeted your career and know what you want to say on your resume. Resume Express makes it easy to enter your information into the computer and with a few keystrokes shape a variety of resumes using different formats and layout structures. **$19.95**

Power Letters ™

A strategic cover letter is one of your best marketing tools to communicate your value-added message directly to an employer. Power Letters (DOS) gives you the right words, phrases, and paragraphs to personalize your communications with employers in a way which gives you a competitive advantage. This easy-to-use software program creates winning letters in a matter of minutes. And that's not all! You also get the right tools to organize and manage your job campaign: a Targeted Employer Database to maintain and update your lists of prospective companies and an Activities Log to keep track of your standing with each contact. In these competitive times, even a perfect resume is not enough to get you an interview. Power Letters will help open doors and make your job campaign a success. **$29.95**